more softies

more softies

22 new friends for you to sew and crochet

VIKING
an imprint of
PENGUIN BOOKS

contents

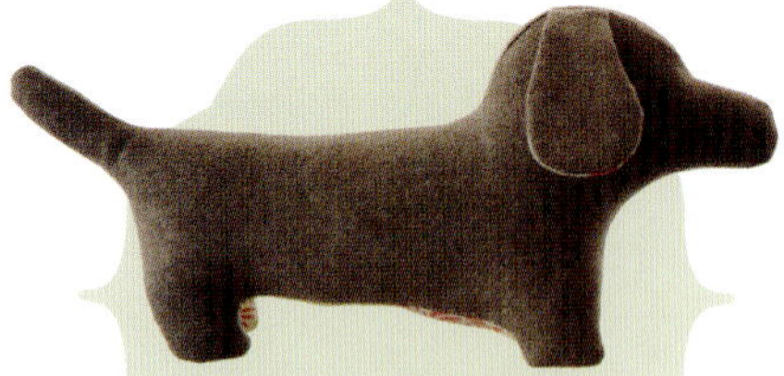

introduction

More Softies is your gateway to the glorious world of homemade soft toys! Hunting down the perfect vintage fabric, choosing which charming toy to make next, and exploring your creativity with new techniques and styles, are all part of the fun of making your own softies. Friends and family will treasure your creations, knowing there is a little of your own personality in every creature you make.

Talented crafters from around the world have contributed their inspired designs to this book and each unique softie is testament to their passion and inventiveness.

Inside, you will find instructions and patterns for 22 original and adorable soft toys that will appeal to adults and children alike. The toys are made using a range of techniques, from simple hand-sewing to crochet, and there are patterns to suit everyone – from complete beginners to experienced crafters. Each entry includes a list of tools and materials that you'll need, as well as detailed instructions, hints and tips.

The instructions are clear and simple, and a handy glossary of terms and techniques ensures that even if you've never felt crafty before, you'll be able to create one of these fabulous critters.

before you start

Before you start, there are a few basic things to note:

- Pre-wash and iron all fabrics before beginning.
- All patterns include a 6 mm (1/4 in) seam allowance. However, note that pieces such as faces, noses and eyes (often made of felt) will usually not have seam allowances, as they don't require them.
- Each pattern specifies how much to enlarge it, in order to make the toy at the size pictured. However, you can enlarge the patterns to whatever size you desire – just remember that your fabric requirements will change.
- When tracing pattern pieces onto tracing paper, be sure to transfer all markings.
- When cutting out body fabric to be sewn together, be sure to pin the template to the right side of the fabric for one of the pieces, and to the wrong side for the other (so you end up with a 'mirrored' set of body shapes). This will ensure the patterned (right) side of the fabric shows when the body is turned right side out.

- Any toys with small parts such as buttons are not suitable for children under three years of age. However, in most instances these components can be substituted with felt, fabric or embroidery.
- The glossary at the back of the book is a quick, handy reference that includes definitions of commonly used terms and abbreviations, as well as explanations of how to do some basic sewing, knitting and crochet stitches.
- Instructions for some of the toys will direct you to pin the pre-sewn arms, legs and/or ears into place on the right side of one body piece, 'pointing in towards the body'. This is so that when you sew the two body pieces together (right sides facing), you will attach the limbs/ears to the body at the same time. It is important to ensure you position the appendages so that they will be facing the right way when the toy is turned right side out (e.g. so that the toes point outwards). The diagram below shows an example of how to pin limbs onto the body correctly. It shows one body piece placed right side up, with limbs pinned on (pointing in towards the body). The next step would be to place the remaining body piece right side down on top, and sew around the body (leaving an opening for turning right side out and stuffing).

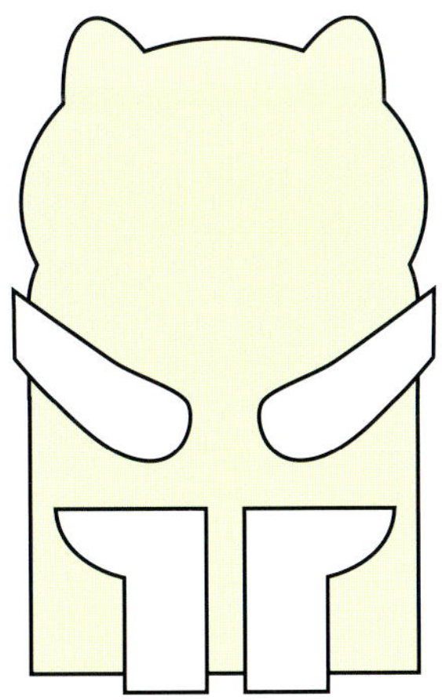

car & caravan

{Hatch – www.prairiemouse.typepad.com} LOUISE HATCHARD

This softie car and its little caravan are all set to head off on an adventure to a magical land – the vines are trimmed, the headlights are shiny, and the flowers are blooming in the window box.

FINISHED SIZE

- Each 10 cm × 13 cm (4 in × 5 in)

TOOLS

- Tracing paper
- Fabric marker
- Scissors
- Pins
- Sewing needle
- 9 cm (3½ in) doll needle
- Sewing machine
- Stuffing stick (or chopstick)
- Iron

MATERIALS

- Car fabric – a piece of 30 cm × 25 cm (12 in × 10 in) patterned fabric (iron a piece of light fusible interfacing onto the back if the fabric is lightweight). (You could also use felt or blanketing if you prefer, and then hand sew the toy using blanket stitch.)
- Caravan fabric – a piece of 30 cm × 25 cm (12 in × 10 in) patterned fabric to contrast with the car (iron a piece of light fusible interfacing onto the back if the fabric is lightweight).
- Extra fabric – small pieces of coloured felt for the caravan door, car and caravan windows, flowers and leaves; fusible web (optional).
- Decorations – six 2.5 cm (1 in) vintage or covered buttons for the wheels; one 15 mm (½ in) flat button, for the tow bar; two 10 mm (⅖ in) buttons for headlights; 1 flower-shaped button for the door handle (optional).
- Thread – coloured sewing thread to match car and caravan fabric; strong linen thread for sewing on buttons; embroidery thread in 4 or 5 colours.
- Stuffing – polyfill.

{CONTINUED}

{car & caravan}

INSTRUCTIONS

1 Trace and cut out the enlarged pattern using the template provided. Pin it to the appropriate fabric and cut out the pieces. You will need to cut 2 car body shapes and 1 of each caravan body shape, 1 car and 1 caravan top shape, 1 car and 1 caravan bottom shape, 1 caravan door, 1 caravan arched window and window box, 1 caravan round window, 2 car side windows, 1 car front window and 1 car back window from your fabric.

2 Pin one car body piece to the car top piece (right sides facing), with long sides aligned. Baste together (don't worry that the top piece is longer than the body piece). Pin the other car body piece to the other long side of the top piece (right sides facing), and baste together. Now trim the excess fabric from the top piece. Machine stitch the top piece to both body pieces, where you have basted.

3 Baste the car bottom piece to the base of the car (right side facing in). This piece will also be a little long, so start by tacking along a long side, then tack across a short side and then along the other long side – you can trim the bottom piece at this stage, then tack along the last short side. Machine stitch the bottom piece to the car body, where you have basted, remembering to leave a gap for turning right side out and stuffing (as marked on the pattern). Unpick the basting along the stuffing opening and turn the car right side out. Use a stuffing stick to stuff the car firmly. Sew the stuffing opening closed using a tiny whip stitch

4 Repeat steps 2 and 3 to make the caravan using the caravan body pieces and the caravan top and bottom pieces.

5 To attach the large buttons (wheels) to the car, thread the doll needle with strong linen thread. For the front wheels of the car, insert the needle at x, coming out on the opposite side of the body. Thread the needle through a hole in a button, then insert the needle into the second hole in the button and push the needle back through the body. Thread the needle through another button, then push the needle back through the body and through each button 2 or 3 more times, pulling the thread taught each time, until the wheels are firmly attached. Repeat at y for the back car wheels and at z for the caravan wheels.

6 Sew the flat button (tow bar) onto the bottom of the car (at o).

7 Cut a 4 cm (1½ in) length of three-strand embroidery thread. Make it into a loop and attach this to the front of the caravan, in the centre of the seam that joins the top caravan piece to the bottom piece. If you wish, sew around the loop using a blanket stitch to strengthen it.

8 Embroider the windows and doors before attaching (my embroidery was done using stem stitch). If you like, use fusible web to position these pieces before using embroidery thread and a tiny blanket stitch to sew them on. Add extra embroidery and decorate with felt flowers and leaves if you want (I have embroidered vines using stem stitch, and attached leaves along the way). Attach the 2 small buttons to the front of the car, for headlights, and sew the flower-shaped button onto the caravan door. Cut out a little rectangle of felt if you would like a number plate, and sew onto the back of the car.

9 Push the tow bar button on the car through the loop on the front of the caravan to link the toys together.

{CONTINUED}

Enlarge template to 200% Seam allowance is included

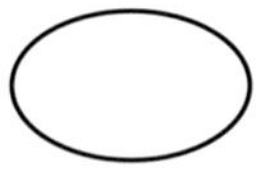

CAR BACK WINDOW
cut 1

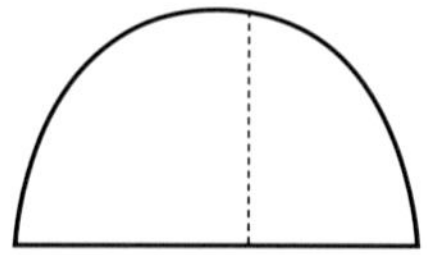

CAR SIDE WINDOW
cut 2

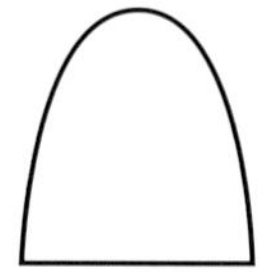

CAR FRONT WINDOW
cut 1

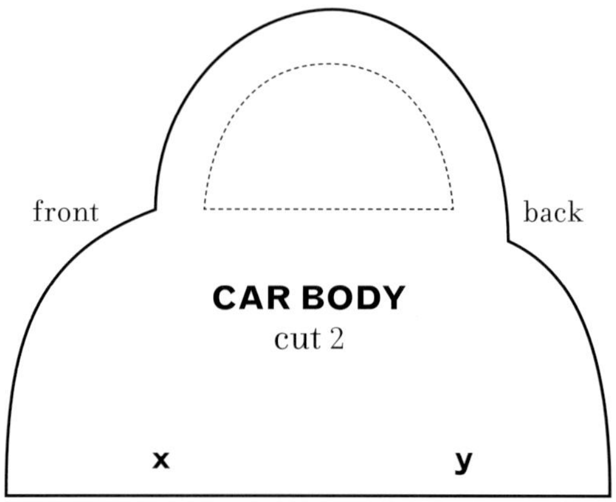

CAR BODY
cut 2

CAR BOTTOM
cut 1

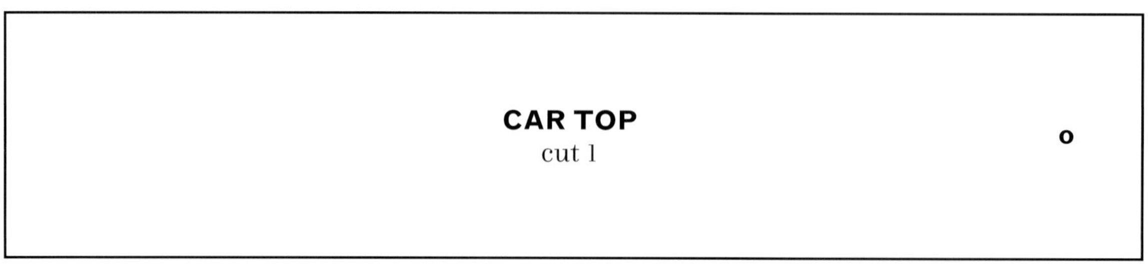

CAR TOP
cut 1

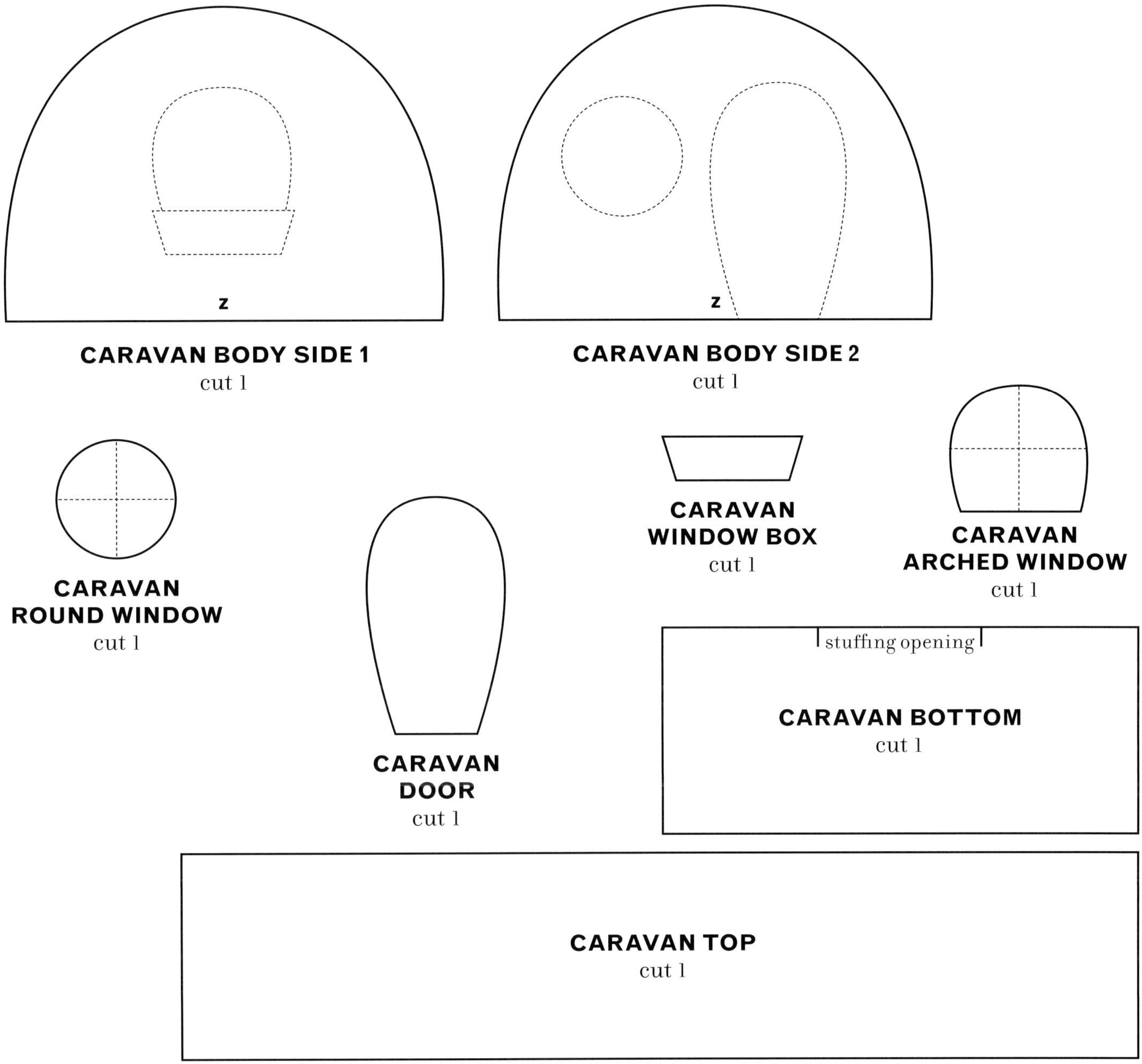
Z
CARAVAN BODY SIDE 1
cut 1
Z
CARAVAN BODY SIDE 2
cut 1
CARAVAN
ROUND WINDOW
cut 1
CARAVAN
DOOR
cut 1
CARAVAN
WINDOW BOX
cut 1
CARAVAN
ARCHED WINDOW
cut 1
stuffing opening
CARAVAN BOTTOM
cut 1
CARAVAN TOP
cut 1

victor giraffe

{www.karkovski.typepad.com} KRISTINA KARKOV

I based this giraffe pattern on a collage I made out of vintage paper. After being inspired by other 'giraffe makers', I decided to turn the design into a three-dimensional toy. This is the result.

FINISHED SIZE

- 26 cm × 10 cm (10 in × 4 in)

TOOLS

- Tracing paper
- Fabric marker
- Scissors
- Pins
- Sewing needle
- Sewing machine
- Stuffing stick (or chopstick)

MATERIALS

- Body fabric – a 30 cm × 40 cm (12 in × 16 in) piece of patterned fabric for the body, and a 21 cm × 25 cm (8½ in × 10 in) piece of the same fabric for the gusset and ears.
- Thread – coloured sewing thread to match fabric; embroidery thread or yarn for the eyes and tail.
- Stuffing – polyfill.

INSTRUCTIONS

1 Trace and cut out the enlarged pattern using the template provided. Pin it to the fabric and cut out the pieces. You will need to cut 2 body shapes, 1 gusset shape and 4 ear shapes from your fabric.

2 Pin the 2 body shapes together (right sides facing) and sew from A to B, around the back, neck and head.

3 Pin the gusset piece to the body piece, A to A and B to B, (right sides facing). Sew together, leaving an opening for turning right side out and stuffing (as marked on the pattern). Clip all curves close to the stitch line to allow for a smoother finish after turning right side out. Turn right side out.

4 Using a stuffing stick, carefully push small amounts of stuffing into the tight corners first – nose, neck and legs. Gradually fill the rest of the body until the stuffing

{CONTINUED}

is firm and even. Hand sew the stuffing opening closed using a whip stitch.

5 For each ear, pin 2 pieces together (right sides facing), then sew, leaving the straight edge open for turning right side out. Turn right side out. Turn the raw edge under 6 mm (¼ in) and hand sew the opening closed using a ladder stitch. Position the ears on the head, folding each slightly at the base (as marked on the pattern), and attach with a ladder stitch.

6 To make the tail, cut three 6 cm (2⅓ in) lengths of embroidery thread or yarn. Attach them to the seam at x, then braid the threads together and tie a knot at the end (see photo on this page).

7 Use embroidery thread to sew the eyes, as follows. Insert the needle at y and push it all the way through the head, coming out on the opposite side, then make a stitch and push it back through the head. Go back and forth through the head a few times so there are several stitches for each eye, pulling the thread tight each time to make the eyes indented. Tie off and hide the thread in the body.

Enlarge template to 200% Seam allowance is included

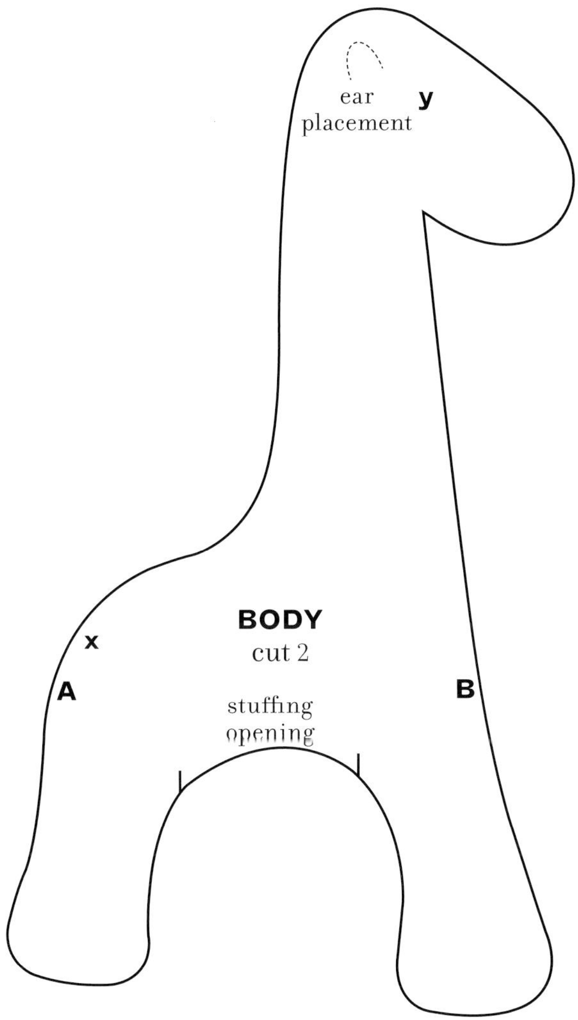

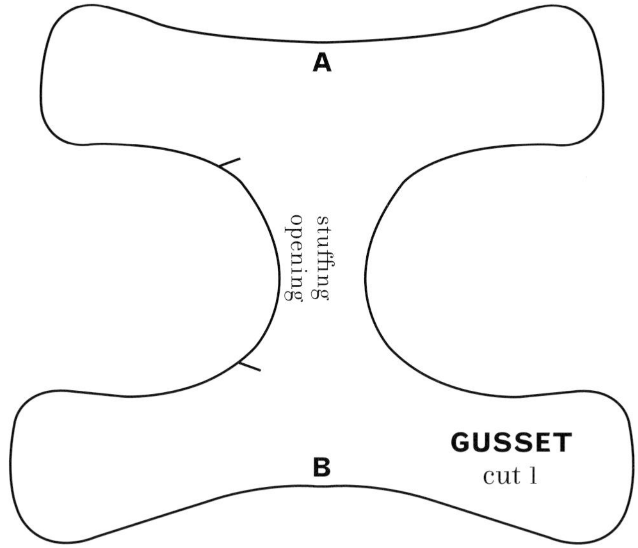

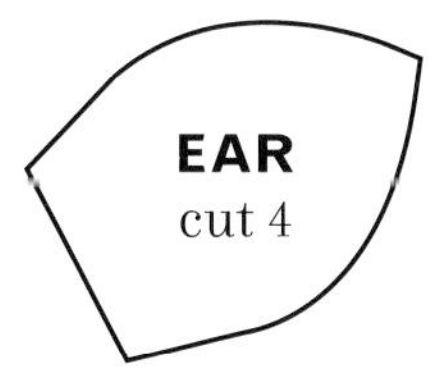

the scream

{Electric Sheep Fiber Arts – amysbabies.etsy.com} AMY J SHIMEL

Why is he screaming? What terrible thing did he see or hear to cause the look of abject horror on his face? *The Scream* painting by Edvard Munch is an icon of the expressionist art movement, and is an artwork that evokes so much emotion in people. This amigurumi version is perfect as a desk buddy or to keep with your art collection. (This pattern is of medium difficulty. Knowledge of increases and decreases and some embroidery is needed.)

FINISHED SIZE

- 13 cm (5 in) × 7 cm (3 in)

TOOLS

- Crochet hook: 1 × 3.5 mm (size E/4)
- Tapestry needle
- Small sewing needle

MATERIALS

- YARN
  Black: 46 metres (50 yards).
  White: 14 metres (15 yards).
- THREAD – Black embroidery thread; white sewing thread.
- STUFFING – plastic pellets and a pinch of polyfill.

ABBREVIATIONS

- **ch** chain
- **sl st** slip stitch
- **dc** double crochet (**sc** single crochet in the US)
- **dc dec** decrease 1 stitch with double crochet (**sc dec** or **sc 2tog** decrease 1 stitch with single crochet in the US)
- ***** indicates beginning of a section to be repeated

{CONTINUED}

{the scream}

NOTES

This doll is worked in the round. Mark the last stitch in each round to keep track of where you are supposed to stop each round. This doll is crocheted with a very tight tension (gauge) – tension is 6 stitches and 6 rows per 2.5 cm (1 in). Tight tension will stop the stuffing from showing through the stitches and help the doll keep its shape. Work through both loops unless instructed otherwise.

Some parts of this doll are started using a self-tightening ring (see instructions on pages 36–37).

INSTRUCTIONS

1 BODY

With black yarn:

R1 6 dc into the ring and pull the ring tight. Mark the last stitch. (6 dc.)

R2 2 dc into each stitch around. (12 dc.)

R3 *1 dc, 2 dc into next stitch, repeat from * 5 more times. (18 dc.)

R4 *2 dc, 2 dc into next stitch, repeat from * 5 more times. (24 dc.)

R5 *3 dc, 2 dc into next stitch, repeat from * 5 more times. (30 dc.)

R6 *4 dc, 2 dc into next stitch, repeat from * 5 more times. (36 dc.)

R7 In back loops only, dc into each stitch around. (36 dc.)

R8 In both loops, dc into each stitch around. (36 dc.)

R9–14 7 dc, dc dec twice, 16 dc, 2 dc into next dc twice, 7 dc. (36 dc.)

R15–18 dc into each stitch around. (36 dc.)

R19–24 7 dc, 2 dc into next dc twice, 16 dc, dc dec twice, 7 dc. (36 dc.)

R25–28 dc into each stitch around. (36 dc.)

R29 *4 dc, dc dec, repeat from * 5 more times. (30 dc.)

R30 *3 dc, dc dec, repeat from * 5 more times. (24 dc.)

R31 *2 dc, dc dec, repeat from * 5 more times. (18 dc.)

R32 *1 dc, dc dec, repeat from * 5 more times. (12 dc.)

R33–35 dc into each stitch around. (12 dc.)

Finish off and leave a tail long enough to use to sew the head onto the body.

2 HEAD

With white yarn:

R1 6 dc into the ring and pull the ring tight. Mark the last stitch. (6 dc.)

R2 2 dc into each stitch around. (12 dc.)
R3–6 dc into each stitch around. (12 dc.)
R7 *1 dc, 2 dc into next stitch, repeat from * 5 more times. (18 dc.)
R8 *2 dc, 2 dc into next stitch, repeat from * 5 more times. (24 dc.)
R9–12 dc into each stitch around. (24 dc.)
R13 *2 dc, dc dec, repeat from * 5 more times. (18 dc.)
R14 *1 dc, dc dec, repeat from * 5 more times. (12 dc.)
R15 dc dec 6 times. (6 dc.)

Finish off and leave a tail long enough to sew the opening in the top of the head closed. Sew the opening closed, hiding the tail and knot inside the head.

3 ARMS

For each arm, with white yarn:
R1 6 dc into the ring and pull the ring tight. Mark the last stitch. (6 dc.)
R2 *2 dc, 2 dc into next stitch, repeat from * once. (8 dc.)
R3 *3 dc, 2 dc into next stitch, repeat from * once. (10 dc.)
R4–8 dc into each stitch around. (10 dc.)
R9 *3 dc, dc dec, repeat from * once. (8 dc.)
R10 *2 dc, dc dec, repeat from * once. (6 dc.)

Continue crocheting around until the arm is 6 cm (2½ in) long. Finish off.

4 At this point you should have an empty body, a head and 2 arms. Fill the body with plastic pellets – you can use the wrong end of a crochet hook to push the pellets into all the curves in the body. The body won't be spherical, but rather flattened on the front and back, with rounded sides. Take a small piece of polyfill and stuff it into the shoulder area to keep the pellets in place. Pinch together the front and back of the neck opening to close it, and sew it closed using the black yarn tail. *Do not cut the tail off yet!*

5 Squeeze the head flat – the chin will be quite flat and the head will be convex (rounded on the front). Using the black embroidery thread, embroider the face onto the head (as shown in the main photograph). Make sure you only sew through one layer of crochet, so the threads don't show on the back of the head. Use French knots to make the pupils.

{CONTINUED}

6 Position the head on the neck – the chin should be about 2.5 cm (1 in) below the top of the neck (see photograph on this page). Using the black tail of yarn, insert your needle through one side of the head and push the needle between the crochet layers of the head so the thread is concealed, coming out horizontally on the other side of the head. Pull tight and tie off. You might also want to take a stitch on the back side of the bottom of the chin, to hold the head at the desired angle. Hide the knot and tail inside the body.

7 Using white sewing thread, sew the hands onto the sides of the face and the body (as shown in the photographs).

twinkles

{H. Luv Fabrications – mciverson.com} HEIDI IVERSON

Twinkles (Girl in a Bear Suit) was based on a painting I did for a solo art show called Polywogadoodle. When I completed the doll version it reminded me of my little sister when she was four years old, so I named it after her. If you don't have a little sister, you need one of these little sister dolls! Sisters are the best things in the world.

FINISHED SIZE

- 22 cm × 16 cm (9 in × 6 in) – excluding limbs

TOOLS

- Tracing paper
- Fabric marker
- Scissors
- Pinking shears
- Pins
- Tapestry needle
- Sewing machine
- 2 × 3.25 mm (US size 3/UK size 10) double-pointed knitting needles
- Stuffing stick (or chopstick)

MATERIALS

- Body fabric – two 20 cm × 30 cm (8 in × 11 in) sheets of felt for the body and ears.
- Extra fabric – a 13 cm × 13 cm (5 in × 5 in) piece of lightweight linen, cotton or felt for the face; scraps of felt in different colours for the eyes, nose and mouth; a 13 cm × 8 cm (5 in × 3 in) piece of felt for the hair.
- Yarn – 46 metres (50 yards) of fingering-weight merino wool or sock yarn, for the arms and legs.
- Thread – coloured sewing thread to match all the fabric colours.
- Stuffing – polyfill.

{CONTINUED}

INSTRUCTIONS

1 Trace and cut out the enlarged pattern using the template provided. Pin it to the appropriate fabric and cut out the pieces. You will need to cut 2 body shapes, 2 ear shapes, 1 nose shape, 1 face shape and 1 hair shape from your fabric. (I never cut out the same hair style twice – cut the fringe freehand and be creative). For the eyes and mouth, choose from the options provided and cut 2 eye shapes and 1 mouth shape. Use scissors to cut out the face, eyes, mouth, nose and hair, and use pinking shears to cut out the body and ears.

2 Pin the face piece onto the head of the body, right side up (as marked on the pattern). Using the sewing machine, zigzag stitch around the face, covering the raw edge of the fabric. Position the hair on the face (as marked) and zigzag around the top (curved) edge only. Position the eyes, nose and mouth on the face and use a straight stitch to sew on using the machine or by hand.

3 The arms and legs are made from 'I-cord', which is knitted with wool or yarn. Start by casting 4 stitches onto your knitting needles. Knit those stitches. Then, instead of turning your work and knitting back the other way, switch the needles in your hands without turning your work. Slide the stitches to the other side of the needle in your left hand – with the yarn still hanging from the left needle, instead of the right, as it usually would – and knit across. Be sure the fabric rolls in on itself, like a tiny little tube.

Keep knitting until the piece measures 10 cm (4 in). Bind off all stitches. You will need to make two 10 cm (4 in) pieces for the arms and two 15 cm (6 in) pieces for the legs (although the arms and legs can really be as long or short as you like). Weave in all ends using the tapestry needle.

4 Place the front body piece wrong side up on your work surface. Fold and pin-tuck the ears, then pin them into position on the body (x to x). Pin the arms onto the body at y, and the legs at z. Place the second body piece wrong side down on top and pin the 2 body pieces together. Sew, using a straight stitch on the machine and leaving a 10 mm ($\frac{2}{5}$ in) seam allowance, securing the limbs and ears in place as you go, and leaving an opening for stuffing (as marked).

{CONTINUED}

5 Using a stuffing stick, push small amounts of stuffing into the small body section first. Then gradually fill the head until the stuffing is firm and even.

6 Hand sew the stuffing opening closed using a straight stitch, or use the sewing machine.

Enlarge template to 200% Seam allowance is included

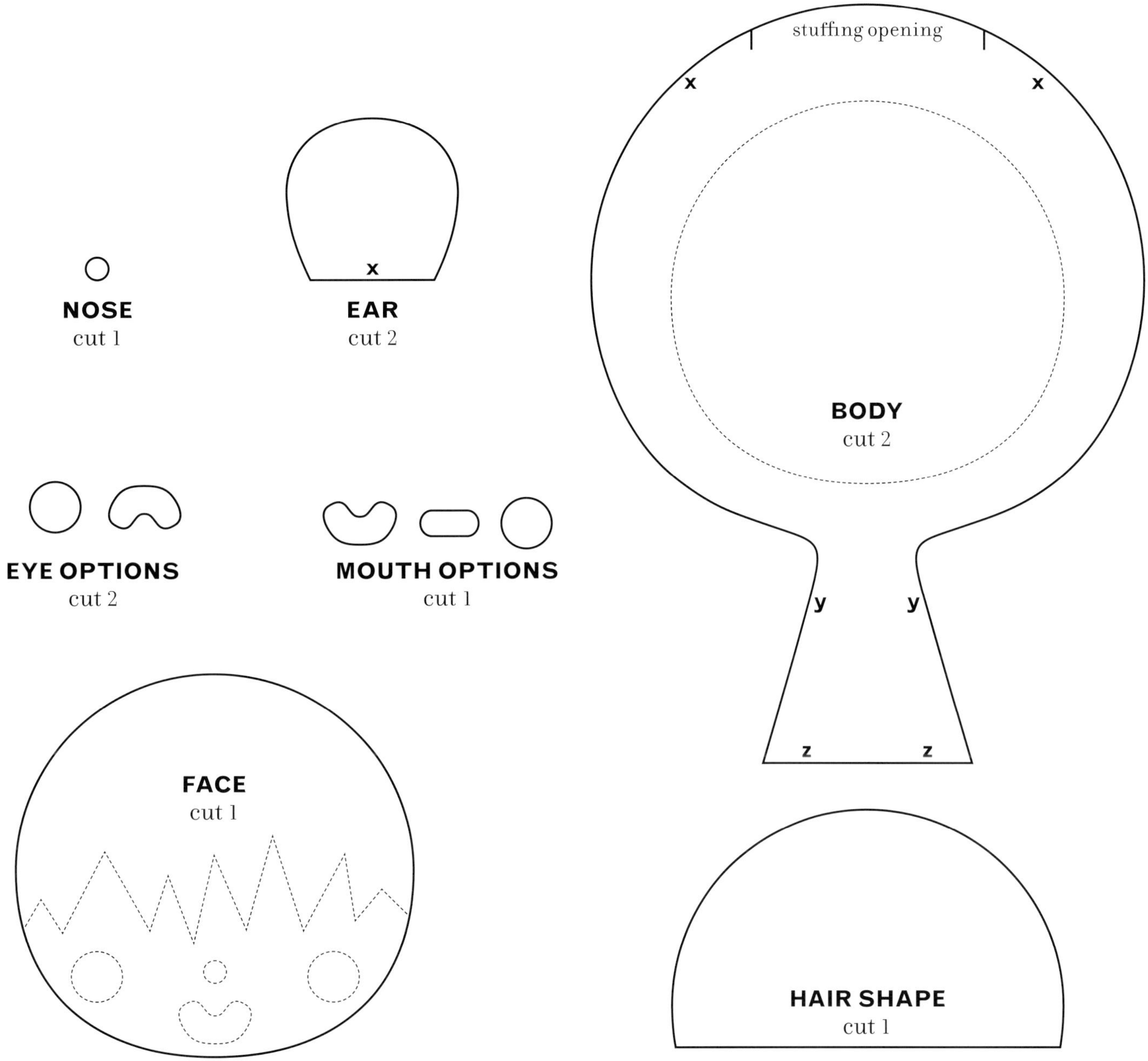

elsie the little dog

{neverenoughhours.blogspot.com} KATE HENDERSON

I first made this little dog for a friend who has a dachshund. The toy is made from wool and cotton fabric. Choose different patterned fabrics to give your sausage dog its own unique personality. (I stitch each seam twice to make it safer for small children.)

FINISHED SIZE

- 14 cm (5½ in) × 33 cm (13 in)

TOOLS

- Tracing paper
- Fabric marker
- Scissors
- Pins
- Sewing needle
- Sewing machine
- Stuffing stick (or chopstick)
- Iron

MATERIALS

- Body fabric – a 40 cm × 38 cm (16 in × 15 in) piece of woollen fabric for the main body, gusset and ears; a 35 cm × 25 cm (14 in × 10 in) piece of patterned cotton for the inner body and insides of the ears.
- Thread – coloured sewing thread to match body fabric; black embroidery thread for the eyes.
- Stuffing – polyfill.

INSTRUCTIONS

1 Trace and cut out the enlarged pattern using the template provided. Pin it to the fabric and cut out the pieces. You will need to cut 2 main body shapes, 2 inner body shapes; 1 gusset shape and 4 ear shapes (2 in patterned fabric and 2 in wool) from your fabric.

2 Using 2 strands of black embroidery thread, satin stitch an eye to each of the main body pieces (as marked on the pattern).

3 For each ear, pin one cotton ear shape to one woollen ear shape (right sides facing), then sew together, leaving the straight edge open for turning right side out. Turn right side out and iron flat. Pin each ear to the wrong side of a main body piece, patterned side up (x to x), pointing in towards the body. Sew in place.

{CONTINUED}

{elsie the little dog}

4 Pin the gusset piece to one of the main body pieces, A to A and B to B, (right sides facing). Sew from A to B. Repeat for the second body piece. (Make sure the ears stay on the right side.) Sew around the nose from A to C, then along the back from B to D.

5 For each inner body piece, sew a dart by folding the leg over (right sides together) then sewing a semi circle (as marked on the pattern). This helps the dog stand up straight. Then pin the 2 inner body pieces together (right sides facing) and sew from C to D along the straighter edge, leaving an opening for turning right side out and stuffing (as marked on the pattern).

6 Pin the inner body piece to the main body piece, C to C and D to D, (right sides facing). Sew from C to D around the legs. Turn the body right side out and iron.

7 Using a stuffing stick, push small amounts of stuffing into the tight corners first – tail, nose and legs. Gradually fill the rest of the body until it is firm and even, but not too tight. Hand stitch the stuffing opening closed using a ladder stitch.

Enlarge template to 200% Seam allowance is included

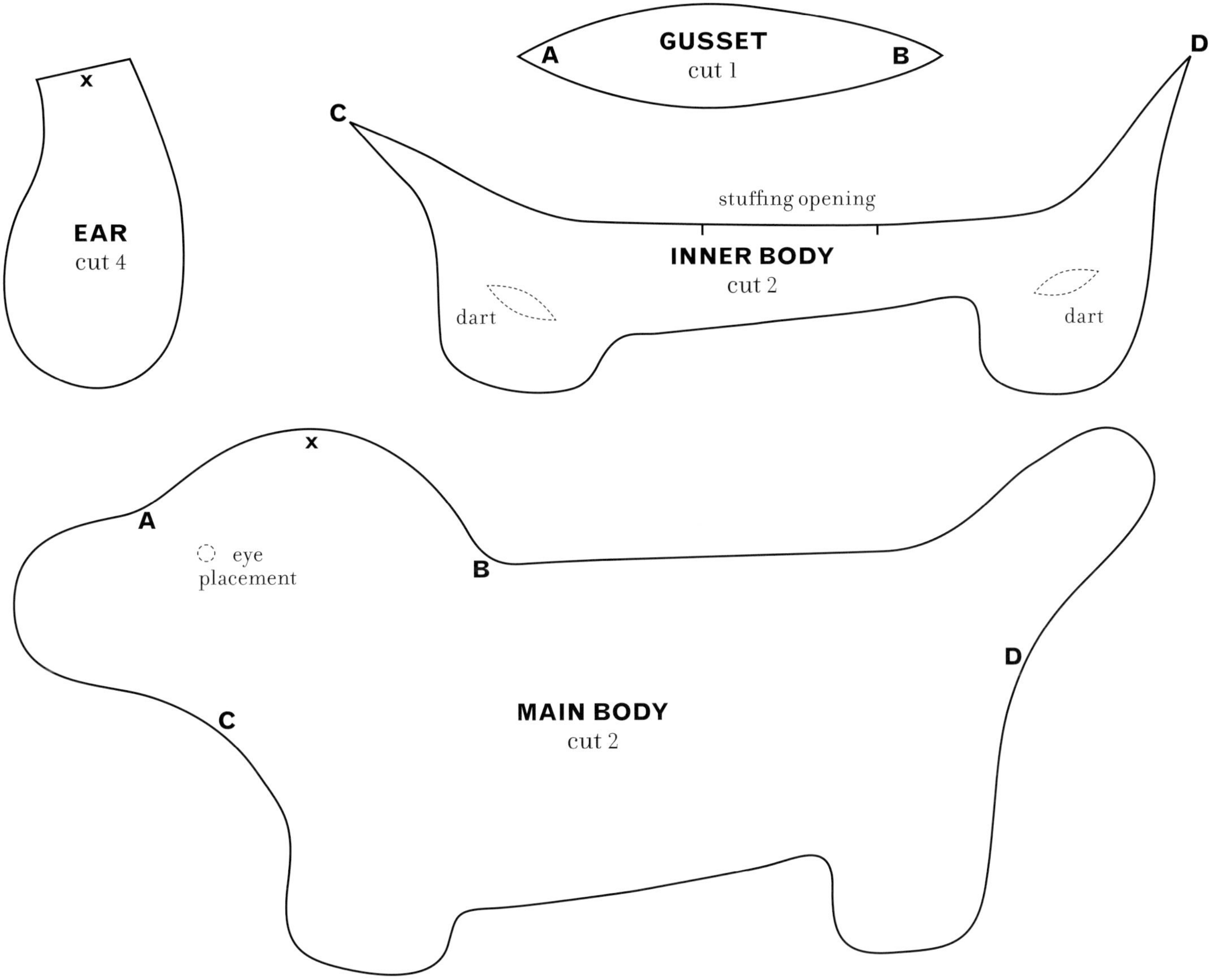

mister rooster

(MariekUniek – www.mariekuniek.com) MARIEKE VAN ESVELD

Animals are a great inspiration for my work, and I like to humanise them a bit. I love to use natural materials like wool felt, cotton and linen – I use fleece as well because of the softness it gives the finished toy. I also like to recycle, so when a piece of clothing isn't worn any more and the fabric is good quality, it frequently ends up in one of my softies (Mister Rooster's trousers are made from my son's old jeans).

FINISHED SIZE

- 35 cm × 28 cm (14 in × 11 in)

TOOLS

- Tracing paper
- Fabric marker
- Scissors
- Pins
- Sewing needle
- Sewing machine
- Stuffing stick (or chopstick)

MATERIALS

- Body fabric – a 15 cm × 50 cm (6 in × 20 in) piece of medium-heavy fabric, such as denim or corduroy, for the trousers; a 20 cm × 30 cm (8 in × 12 in) piece of off-white felt, for the head; a 20 cm × 30 cm (8 in × 12 in) piece of green felt for the body.
- Extra fabric – a 20 cm × 30 cm (8 in × 12 in) piece of grey or black felt for the wings and feet; a 20 cm × 20 cm (8 in × 8 in) piece of red felt for the comb, lobes and cheeks (I used a lighter shade of red for the small lobe and cheeks, for contrast); a scrap of yellow felt, for the beak.
- Thread – coloured sewing thread to match fabric, plus black for the eyes.
- Stuffing – polyfill or wool rovings.

{CONTINUED}

{mister rooster}

INSTRUCTIONS

1 Trace and cut out the enlarged pattern using the template provided. Pin it to the appropriate fabric and cut out the pieces. (Do not cut out the wings and comb yet.) You will need to cut 2 head shapes, 2 body shapes, 2 trousers shapes, 2 toes shapes, 2 cheek shapes, 1 top and 1 bottom lobe shape and 1 beak shape from your fabric.

2 The wings and comb are sewn before they are cut out. Pin a wing pattern piece onto a folded piece of fabric (as marked on the pattern). Use a straight stitch to sew all the way around the template from A to B, leaving an opening for stuffing (as marked), then cut out the shape and cut along the fold. Repeat for the other wing. Make the comb in the same way, sewing from C to D. Stuff each wing and the comb, then stitch the stuffing opening closed. Make sure to leave the 10 mm overhang on the straight edges (as marked on the pattern) for attaching the parts to the body.

3 Pin one of the head pieces to one of the body pieces, E to E and F to F, so it overlaps by 6 mm (¼ in). Sew from E to F, using a tight zigzag stitch. Pin the remaining head and body piece together in the same way, then pin the top and bottom lobes to the right side of the body piece (as marked on the pattern). Sew from E to F, securing the lobes as you go.

4 Pin the beak piece to this stitched piece (as marked on the pattern) and sew on using a tight zigzag stitch: sew around the beak from G to H, then without removing the needle from the fabric, use your scissors or a stuffing stick to push a small amount of stuffing into the beak. Then finish sewing around the beak.

5 To make each nostril on the beak, start with the widest zigzag size and make a few stitches, then choose a smaller zigzag size and sew a few more stitches. Repeat again with a smaller stitch size, then secure and finish off.

6 Pin the cheeks to the face (as marked on the pattern) and sew them on using a zigzag stitch. Pin the toe pieces to the legs of the front body piece (as marked) and sew around the toes using zigzag stitch.

7 Pin each body/head piece to one of the trouser pieces (I to I and J to J), overlapping 6 mm (¼ in). Sew each together using a zigzag stitch.

8 Place the front body piece right side up on your work surface. Place the wings and comb in position (A to A and C to C), pointing in towards the body. Place the second body piece right side down on top and pin the 2 body pieces together. Sew, using a straight stitch, securing the wings and comb in place as you go, and leaving an opening for turning right side out and stuffing (as marked). Trim if necessary and nick fabric around the curved edges, being careful not to clip the seam. Turn right side out.

9 Using a stuffing stick, push small amounts of stuffing into the body until it is firm and even, but still a bit soft.

10 Hand sew the stuffing opening closed using a whip stitch.

{CONTINUED}

Enlarge template to 200% Seam allowance is included

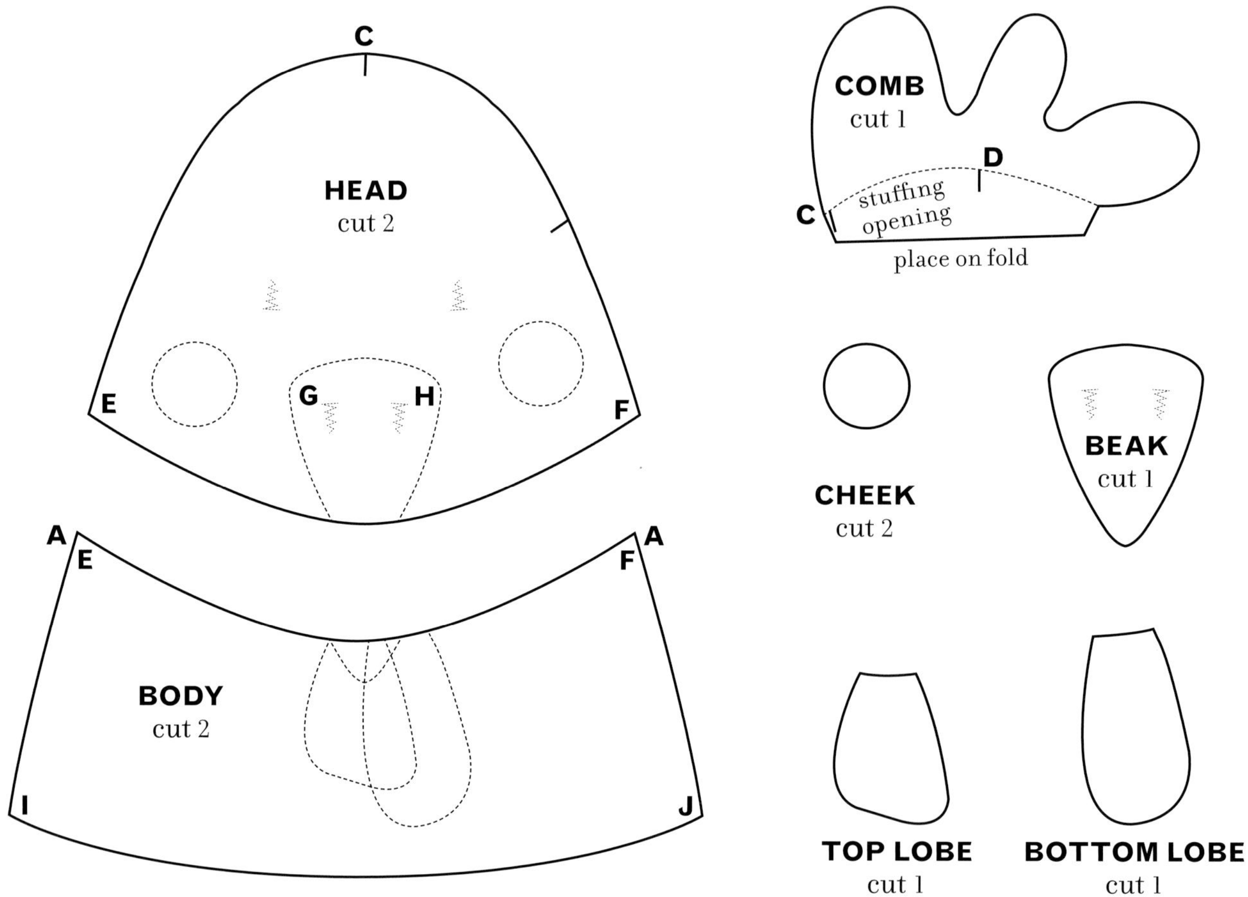

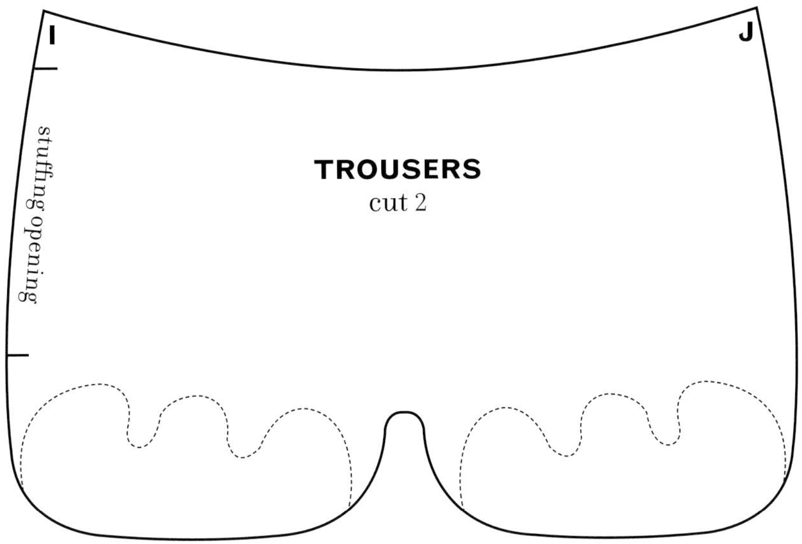
I
J
stuffing opening
TROUSERS
cut 2

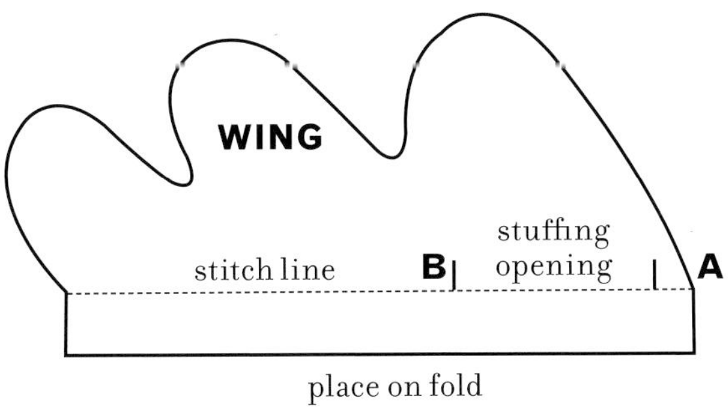
WING
stitch line
B
stuffing
opening
A
place on fold

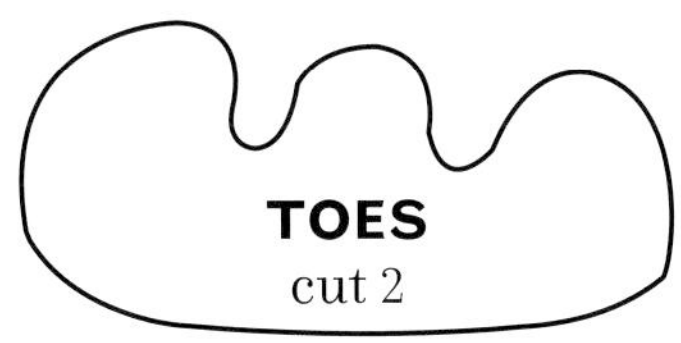
TOES
cut 2

dog & frog rattles

{Soozs – www.soozs.blogspot.com} SUZIE FRY

I developed these toys to appeal to babies, but I find my five-year-old daughter likes them too. With babies in mind, they have rattle inserts, prominent eyes, and ears and noses that are just right for pulling, sucking and chewing. They are easy to hold, fully washable – and best of all, simple to make! I've used 4-ply cotton yarn for the dog and 8-ply cotton yarn for the frog, so you can see what sizes the different yarns produce, but you could use any weight you like for either pattern.

FINISHED SIZE

- Dog (4-ply cotton): 14 cm × 6 cm (5½ in × 2 in)
- Frog (8-ply cotton): 17 cm × 7 cm (7 in × 3 in)

TOOLS

- Scissors
- Pins
- Tapestry needle
- Wool needle
- Crochet hooks: 1 × 2.5 mm for 4 ply; 3.5 mm for 8 ply (or adjust size for your chosen yarn weight, to produce a dense fabric)
- Stuffing stick (or chopstick)

MATERIALS

- **YARN**
  Dog: one 50-g ball 4-ply dark-brown (I used Rowan's Cotton Glace in chocolate).
  Frog: one 50-g ball 8-ply green (I used Twilley's Freedom Cotton DK).
  Both: a small amount of white for the eyes (I used 4-ply Rowan's Cotton Glace, but if you make the frog in 4 ply you'll need to use a finer weight cotton in 2 ply).
- **EMBROIDERY THREAD**
  Dog: small amounts of black and grey.
  Frog: small amounts of black.
- **STUFFING** – polyfill or similar. (Remember that the stuffing material will determine washability – although I generally stuff with wool, I chose a more robust polyester for these rattles.) One rattle insert per toy. (Rattle inserts can be hard to find, but try craft and doll-making suppliers. Alternatively: use any small plastic container and put a bell or some beads inside; use the caged bells sold for cat toys; or cannibalise a cheap rattling toy from the op shop.)

{CONTINUED}

{dog & frog rattles}

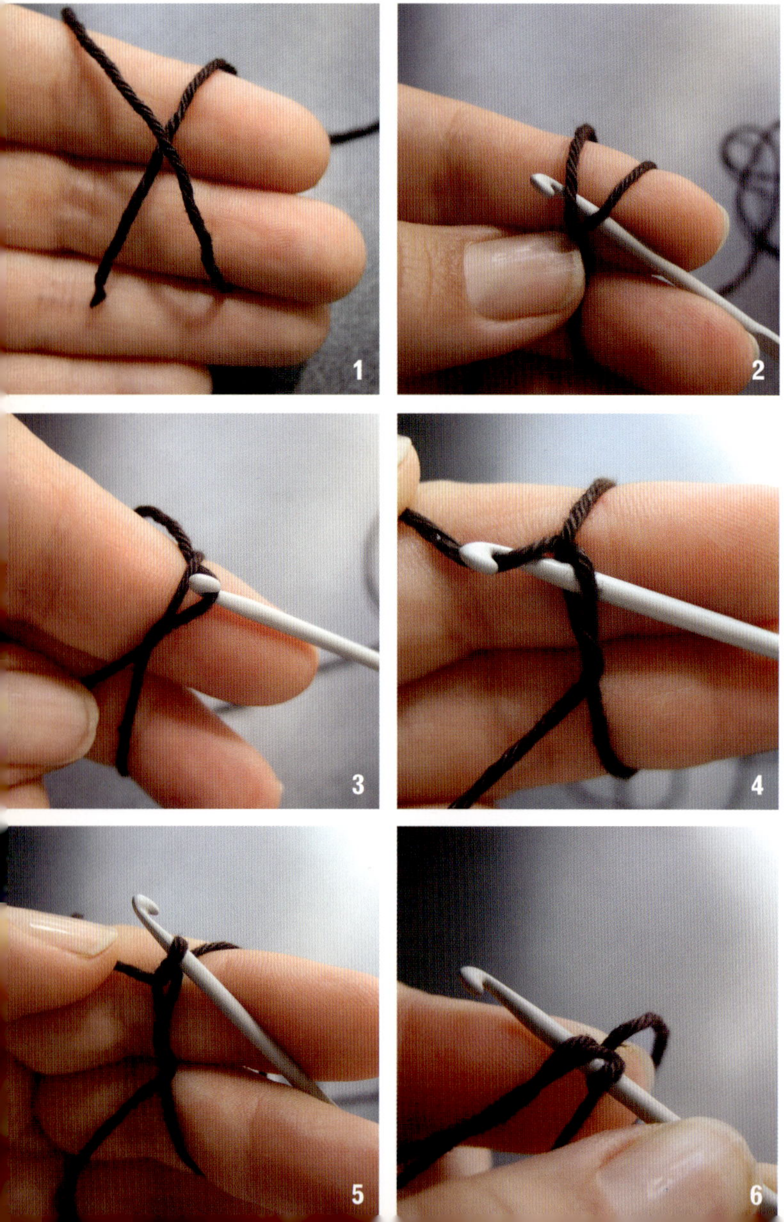

ABBREVIATIONS

- **ch** chain
- **sl st** slip stitch
- **dc** double crochet (**sc** single crochet in the US)
- * indicates beginning of a section to be repeated

NOTES

Some parts of this doll are started using a self-tightening ring. Here are the instructions if you are not familiar with this technique (and see corresponding photographs):

Take your yarn and, holding the tail end between your thumb and forefinger, loop the yarn over, around and under your first 2 fingers so the yarn crosses over the tail and the cross is held under your thumb and forefinger (step 1). Insert your hook from front to back under the loop above your fingers, hook over your yarn (step 2) and pull through under the loop (step 3). You will now have one loop on the hook. Yarn over the hook again (step 4) and pull through the loop (step 5). You are now ready to commence your first double crochet. Insert the hook into the ring again, yarn over again and pull through. You will now have two loops on the hook (step 6). Yarn over again and pull through both loops.

This forms the first double crochet in the ring (step 7). Do 5 more double crochets (step 8), then pull the tail end of the yarn tight (step 9), so the stitches form a circle (step 10). Slip stitch into the first double crochet (step 11), so you have 6 stitches in a ring (step 12).

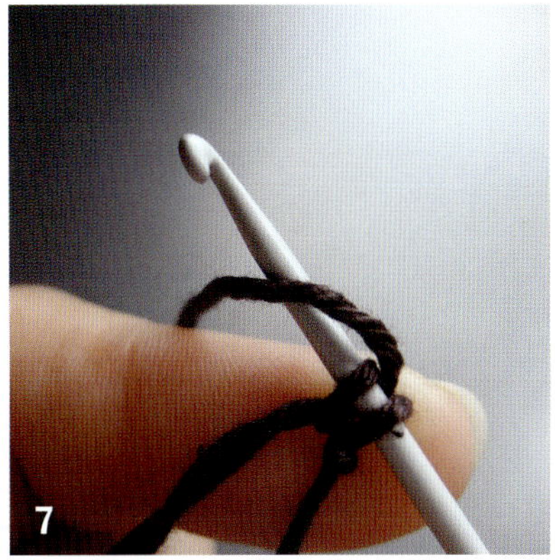

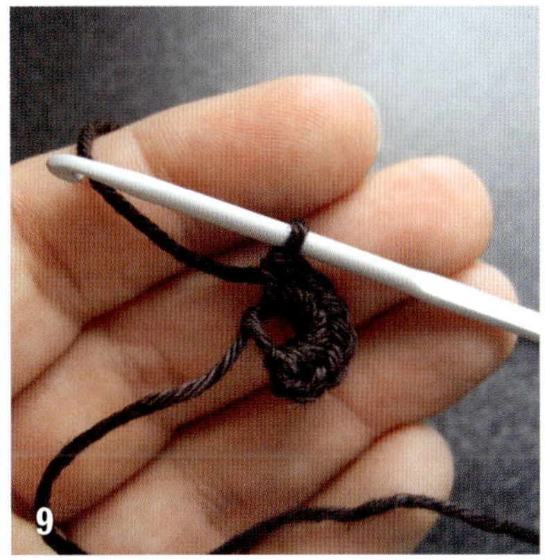

INSTRUCTIONS

1 BODY (THIS IS THE SAME FOR EITHER THE DOG OR FROG)

With body colour (brown or green yarn) and worked from the top down:

R1 Using a self-tightening ring, 6 dc into the centre and sl st to form a ring.

R2 2 dc into each stitch. (12 dc.)

R3 *1 dc into next stitch, 2 dc into following stitch, repeat from * 5 more times. (18 dc.)

R4 *1 dc into next 2 stitches, 2 dc into following stitch, repeat from * 5 more times. (24 dc.)

R5 *1 dc into next 3 stitches, 2 dc into following stitch, repeat from * 5 more times. (30 dc.)

R6 *1 dc into next 5 stitches, 2 dc into following stitch, repeat from * 5 more times. (36 dc.)

R7 *1 dc into next 6 stitches, 2 dc into following stitch, repeat from * 5 more times. (42 dc.)

R8–15 1 dc into each stitch. (42 dc.)

{CONTINUED}

R16 *1 dc into each of the next 5 stitches, decrease 1 stitch by inserting hook into next stitch, yarn over and pull through, leaving 2 loops on the hook. Insert the hook into next stitch, yarn over and pull through, leaving 3 loops on hook. Yarn over and pull through all 3 loops. Repeat from * 5 more times. (36 stitches.)

R17 *1 dc into each of the next 4 stitches, decrease 1 stitch by inserting hook into next stitch, yarn over and pull through, leaving 2 loops on the hook. Insert the hook into next stitch, yarn over and pull through, leaving 3 loops on hook. Yarn over and pull through all 3 loops. Repeat from * 5 more times. (30 stitches.)

R18 *1 dc into each of the next 3 stitches, decrease 1 stitch by inserting hook into next stitch, yarn over and pull through, leaving 2 loops on the hook. Insert the hook into next stitch, yarn over and pull through, leaving 3 loops on hook. Yarn over and pull through all 3 loops. Repeat from * 5 more times. (24 stitches.)

R19 * 1 dc into each of the next 2 stitches, decrease 1 stitch by inserting hook into next stitch, yarn over and pull through, leaving 2 loops on the hook. Insert the hook into next stitch, yarn over and pull through, leaving 3 loops on hook. Yarn over and pull through all 3 loops. Repeat from * 5 more times. (18 stitches.)

Insert a thick layer of stuffing into the top and sides of the head, place rattle insert in the centre, then firmly stuff the head.

R20–34 1 dc into each stitch. (18 dc.)

R35 *1 dc into next 5 stitches, 2 dc into following stitch, repeat from * 3 more times. (21 dc.)

R36 *1 dc into next 6 stitches, 2 dc into following stitch, repeat from * 3 more times. (24 dc.)

R37 *1 dc into next 7 stitches, 2 dc into following stitch, repeat from * 3 more times. (27 dc.)

R38 *1 dc into next 8 stitches, 2 dc into following stitch, repeat from * 3 more times. (30 dc.)

R39 1 dc into each stitch. (30 dc.)

R40 *1 dc into each of the next 3 stitches, decrease 1 stitch by inserting hook into next stitch, yarn over and pull through, leaving 2 loops on the hook. Insert the hook into next stitch, yarn over and pull through, leaving 3 loops on hook. Yarn over and pull through all 3 loops. Repeat from * 5 more times. (24 stitches.)

R41 *1 dc into each of the next 2 stitches, decrease 1 stitch by inserting hook into next stitch, yarn over and pull through, leaving 2 loops on the hook. Insert the hook into next stitch, yarn over and pull through, leaving 3 loops on hook. Yarn over and pull through all 3 loops. Repeat from * 5 more times. (18 dc.)

Stuff the rattle handle firmly, pushing stuffing all the way up to the head to make sure the rattle insert remains centred in the head.

R42 *1 dc into next stitch, decrease 1 stitch by inserting hook into next stitch, yarn over and pull through, leaving 2 loops on the hook. Insert the hook into next stitch, yarn over and pull through, leaving 3 loops on hook. Yarn over and pull through all 3 loops. Repeat from * 5 more times. (12 stitches.)

R43 *Decrease 1 stitch by inserting hook into next stitch, yarn over and pull through, leaving 2 loops on the hook. Insert the hook into next stitch, yarn over and pull through, leaving 3 loops on hook. Yarn over and pull through all 3 loops. Repeat from * 5 more times. (6 stitches.)

Fill any space with extra stuffing, then using the wool needle, sew in tail of yarn and close hole.

From this point, follow the step numbers for the rattle you are making (dog or frog). Dog instructions are below, frog instructions start from step 2 (Frog Mouth) on page 41.

2 DOG SNOUT

With brown yarn and worked from the top down:

R1 Using a self-tightening ring, 6 dc into the centre and sl st to form a ring.

R2 2 dc into each of the next 4 stitches, 1 dc into each of the next 2 stitches. (10 dc.)

R3 *1 dc into the next stitch, 2 dc into the following stitch, repeat from * 3 more times, then 1 dc into each of the next 2 stitches. (14 dc.)

R4 *1 dc into each of the next 2 stitches, 2 dc into the next stitch, repeat from * 3 more times, then 1 dc into each of the next 2 stitches. (18 dc.)

R5 1 dc into each stitch. (18 dc.)

R6 1 dc into each of the next 2 stitches, *1 dc into each of the next 2 stitches, 2 dc into the next stitch, repeat from * 4 more times, then 1 dc into the next stitch. (23 dc.)

R7 1 dc into each stitch. (23 dc.)

R8 1 dc into each stitch. (23 dc.)

Leave a tail on the yarn long enough to sew the snout on, then slip the yarn through the last stitch and pull tight.

{CONTINUED}

3 DOG EARS

With brown yarn and worked from the bottom up (make 2):

R1 Using a self-tightening ring, 6 dc into the centre and sl st to form a ring.

R2 2 dc into each stitch. (12 dc.)

R3 *1 dc into each of the next 3 stitches, 2 dc into the following stitch, repeat from * 2 more times. (15 dc.)

R4 1 dc into each stitch. (15 dc.)

R5 1 dc into each stitch. (15 dc.)

R6 *1 dc into each of the next 3 stitches, decrease 1 stitch by inserting hook into next stitch, yarn over and pull through, leaving 2 loops on the hook. Insert the hook into next stitch, yarn over and pull through, leaving 3 loops on hook. Yarn over and pull through all 3 loops. Repeat from * 2 more times. (12 stitches.)

R7 1 dc into each stitch. (12 dc.)

R8 *1 dc into each of the next 2 stitches, decrease 1 stitch by inserting hook into next stitch, yarn over and pull through, leaving 2 loops on the hook. Insert the hook into next stitch, yarn over and pull through, leaving 3 loops on hook. Yarn over and pull through all 3 loops. Repeat from * 2 more times. (9 stitches.)

R9 1 dc into each stitch. (9 dc.)

R10 *1 dc into next stitch, decrease 1 stitch by inserting hook into next stitch, yarn over and pull through, leaving 2 loops on the hook. Insert the hook into next stitch, yarn over and pull through, leaving 3 loops on hook. Yarn over and pull through all 3 loops. Repeat from * 2 more times. (6 stitches.)

R11 1 dc into each stitch. (6 dc.)

Leave a tail on the yarn long enough to sew the ear on, then slip the yarn through the last stitch and pull tight.

4 DOG EYES

With white yarn and worked from the bottom up (make 2):

R1 Using a self-tightening ring, 6 dc into the centre and sl st to form a ring.

R2 *1 dc into the next stitch, 2 dc into following stitch, repeat from * 2 more times. (9 dc.)

R3 *1 dc into each of the next 2 stitches, 2 dc into following stitch, repeat from * 2 more times. (12 dc.)

Leave a tail on the yarn long enough to sew the eye on, then slip the yarn through the last stitch and pull tight.

5 FINISHING THE DOG

Using black or grey embroidery thread, embroider pupils in the centre of the eyes, a nose on the snout and a mouth line along the underside of the snout.

Sew the tops of the ears in place on either side of the head, just under the third line of crochet stitches from the centre top.

Sew the snout in place so that the bottom of the snout meets the line of decreases as the head becomes the handle of the rattle. When about half sewn on, fill the snout with a little stuffing so it is firm, then finish sewing up.

Sew the eyes on either side of the head, just above the snout.

2 FROG MOUTH

With green yarn and worked from the lips back:
ch 15 stitches.

R1 Starting from the second chain from the hook, 1 dc into top loop of each chain (14 dc), then turn the work

{CONTINUED}

in the round and 1 dc into each of the lower loops of the chain (14 dc). Join with a sl st to form a round. (Total 28 stitches).

R2 2 dc into each of the next 2 stitches, 1 dc into each of the next 12 stitches, 2 dc into each of the next 2 stitches, 1 dc into each of the next 12 stitches, close the round with a sl st. (32 stitches.)

R3 2 dc into each of the next 3 stitches, 1 dc into each of the next 12 stitches, 2 dc into each of the next 3 stitches, 1 dc into each of the next 14 stitches, close the round with a sl st. (38 stitches.)

R4 2 dc into each of the next 4 stitches, 1 dc into each of the next 14 stitches, 2 dc into each of the next 4 stitches, 1 dc into each of the next 16 stitches, close the round with a sl st. (46 stitches.)

R5 2 dc into each of the next 5 stitches, 1 dc into each of the next 16 stitches, 2 dc into each of the next 5 stitches, 1 dc into each of the next 20 stitches, close the round with a sl st. (56 stitches.)

Leave a tail on the yarn long enough to sew the mouth on, then slip the yarn through the last stitch and pull tight.

3 FROG EYELIDS

With green yarn and worked from the top down (make 2):

R1 Using a self-tightening ring, 6 dc into the centre and sl st to form a ring.

R2 2 dc into each stitch. (12 dc.)

R3 *1 dc into next stitch, 2 dc into following stitch, repeat from * 5 more times. (18 dc.)

R4 1 dc into each stitch. (18 dc.)

R5 1 dc into each stitch. (18 dc.)

Leave a tail on the yarn long enough to sew the eyelid on, then slip the yarn through the last stitch and pull tight.

4 FROG EYES

With white yarn and worked from the top down (make 2):

R1 Using a self-tightening ring, 6 dc into the centre and sl st to form a ring.

R2 2 dc into each stitch. (12 dc.)

R3 1 dc into each stitch. (12 dc.)

R4 1 dc into each stitch. (12 dc.)

R5 *Decrease 1 stitch by inserting hook into next stitch, yarn over and pull through, leaving 2 loops on the hook. Insert the hook into the next stitch, yarn over and pull through, leaving 3 loops on hook. Yarn over and pull through all 3 loops. Repeat from * 5 more times. (6 stitches.)

Leave a tail on the yarn long enough to sew the eye on, then slip the yarn through the last stitch and pull tight.

5 FINISHING THE FROG

Using black embroidery thread, sew a line of back stitching across the centre of the mouth to mark the lips (use the initial chain starting line as a guide).

Embroider 2 stitches on the upper side of the mouth (the narrower side) to make nostrils.

Sew the mouth in place on the head so that the bottom of the mouth meets the line of decreases as the head becomes the shaft of the rattle. When about three quarters is sewn on, fill the mouth with stuffing so it is firm and prominent, then finish sewing up.

Flatten the eyelids in half with the beginning point of the crochet at the top. Sew the eyes into the lids and then sew onto the head just above and on either side of the mouth.

Use black embroidery thread to sew one long stitch for each pupil.

{CONTINUED}

circus elephant

{While She Naps – www.whileshenaps.typepad.com} ABIGAIL PATNER GLASSENBERG

This adorable elephant is easy to make and offers lots of opportunity to explore your creativity. Select matching or contrasting fabrics for the ears and legs and choose colourful vintage buttons to attach the legs to the body. Have fun quilting the ears in a unique design. Make multiple elephants and line them up trunk-to-tail for a circus parade!

FINISHED SIZE

- 20 cm × 20 cm (8 in × 8 in)

TOOLS

- Tracing paper (I use freezer paper because you can iron it to the fabric so you don't need to pin)
- Fabric marker
- Scissors
- Pins
- Sewing needle
- 13 cm (5 in) doll needle
- Sewing machine
- Stuffing stick (I use surgical forceps)
- Iron
- Hole puncher
- Small sharp scissors

MATERIALS

- Body fabric – a 40 cm × 46 cm (16 in × 18 in) piece of sturdy woollen or cotton fabric.
- Extra fabric – small pieces of patterned cotton fabric for the ears and legs; a scrap of wool felt for the eyes; small pieces of quilt batting for the ears.
- Decorations – 4 matching buttons, for attaching the legs.
- Thread – sewing thread in matching or contrasting colours; extra-strong sewing thread for attaching the buttons.
- Stuffing – polyfill.

{CONTINUED}

{circus elephant}

INSTRUCTIONS

1 Trace and cut out the enlarged pattern using the template provided. Pin (or iron) it to the appropriate fabric and cut out the pieces. You will need to cut 2 body shapes, 4 ear shapes and 8 leg shapes from your fabric.

2 Pin the 2 body pieces together (wrong sides facing), and sew with a short straight stitch on the sewing machine, remembering to leave an opening for stuffing (as marked on the pattern). These stitches will show on the finished toy, so take your time and make it as neat as possible. Using a pair of small sharp sewing scissors, trim around the elephant's body, about 6 mm (¼ in) from the seam.

3 Use a stuffing stick to stuff the elephant (be patient, as this process takes time and the finished toy should be quite firmly stuffed). Start by inserting a tiny bit of stuffing through the stuffing opening and push it all the way to the tip of the trunk. Repeat until the trunk is stuffed firmly. Continue to stuff the elephant, taking care around the mouth to avoid wrinkles, until the toy is stuffed to your liking. Leave a little room near the stuffing opening for inserting the tail later.

4 For each leg, pin 2 leg shapes together (right sides facing), and sew with the sewing machine, leaving an opening for turning right side out and stuffing (as marked on the pattern). Turn legs right side out. Stuff each leg firmly, then close the stuffing opening using a neat ladder stitch.

5 For each ear, pin 2 ear shapes together (right sides facing) and a piece of quilt batting that is slightly larger than the ear pieces. Sew, leaving an opening for turning right side out (as marked on the pattern). Turn ears right side out, so the batting is on the inside, and iron flat. Turn the raw edges under and iron. Close the opening using a neat ladder stitch. If desired, quilt the ears, either by hand or using a running stitch on the sewing machine.

6 To make the tail, cut a 5 cm x 8 cm (2 in x 3 in) strip of fabric from the leftover body fabric. Add a line of decorative stitching along one long edge if you'd like, and/or fray one edge. Iron a 6 mm (¼ in) hem on one of the short edges. Beginning at the other short edge, roll up the tail until you reach the hem. Hand sew along the hemline using a neat ladder stitch to secure. Insert the tail into the body opening, with the decorative stitching or frayed edge furthest from the body. Pin in place, then sew the body closed using a small back stitch, securing the tail as you go.

7 Pin the ears to the elephant's body (as marked on the pattern). Using a neat ladder stitch and matching thread, stitch along one side of each ear to secure it to the body, and then along the other side, so that the finished ear sticks out at a right angle from the body.

8 Use the hole puncher to punch 2 rounds from a scrap of dark wool felt, for the eyes. Sew eyes onto the body (as marked on the pattern) with a small straight stitch in the centre of each eye.

9 To attach the legs to the body, thread the doll needle with a 46 cm (18 in) length of extra-strong sewing thread. For the back legs, insert the needle through the back of one leg (at x), come up through the front of the leg and then through a hole in a decorative button. Pass the needle back through the second hole in the button and through the leg. Then insert the needle into the body (at x), coming out on the opposite side of the body. Push the needle through the second leg (at x), through another decorative button and back through the button and leg. Push the needle back through the body and through each leg and button 2 or 3 more times, pulling the thread taught each time, until the legs are securely attached to the body. Tie off the thread with a double knot underneath one leg so that the stray threads are hidden. Repeat for the front legs.

{CONTINUED}

Template shown at 100% Seam allowance is included

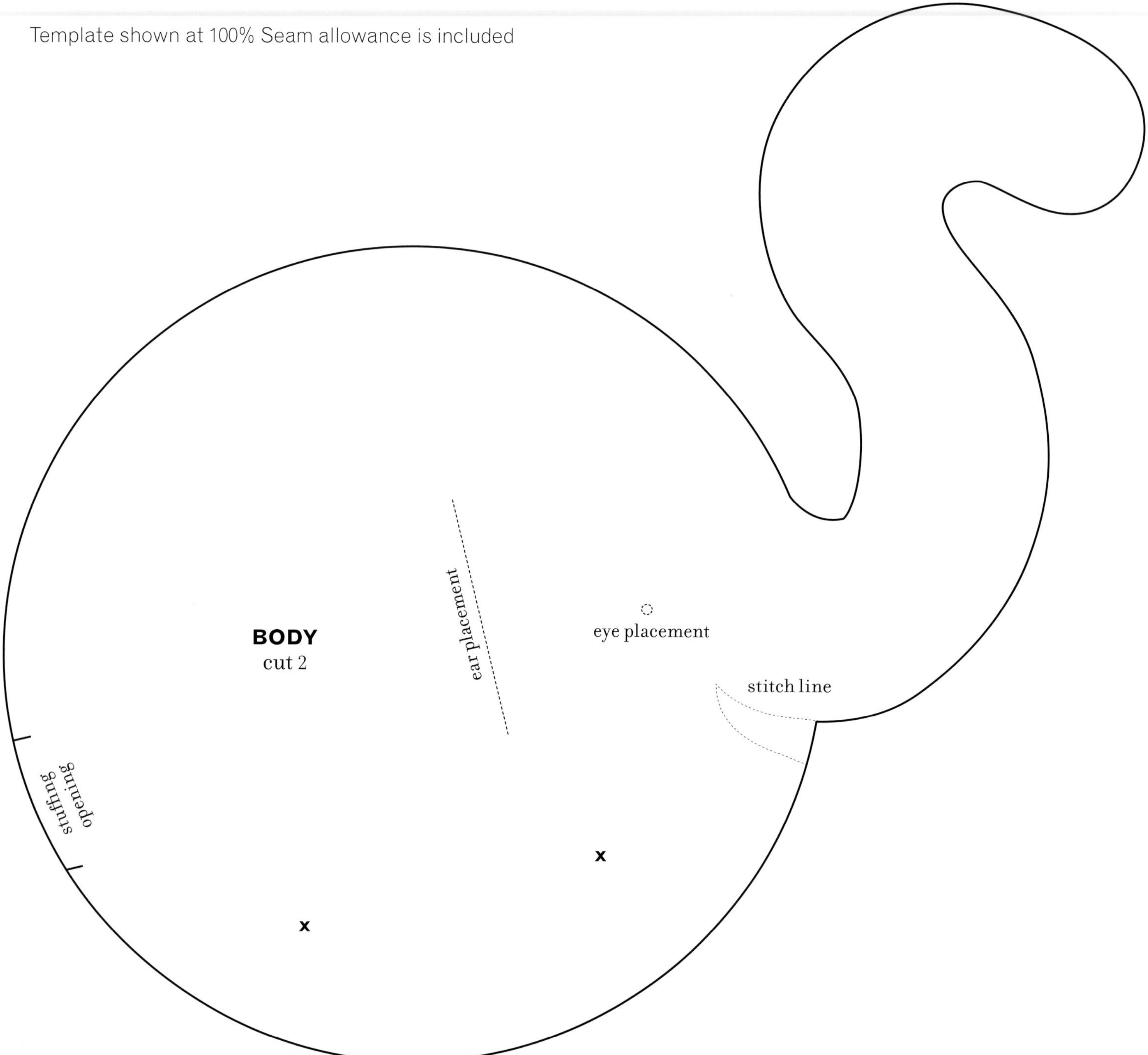

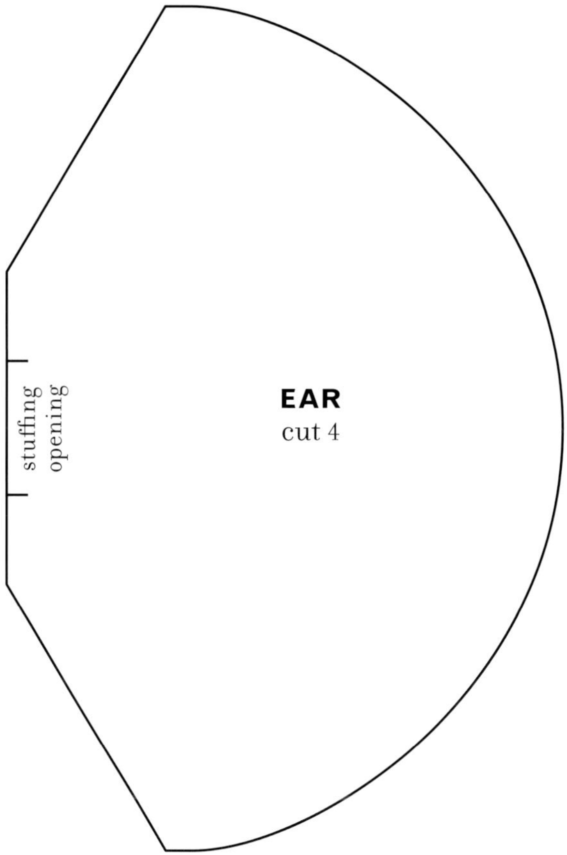
EAR
cut 4
stuffing opening

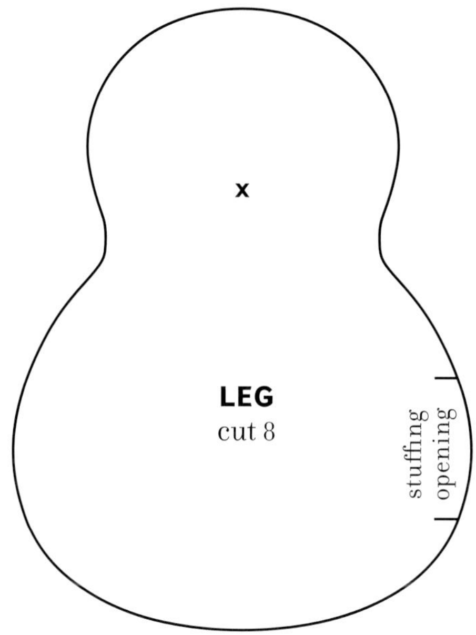
x
LEG
cut 8
stuffing opening

smirky

{herzensart – www.herzensart.com} SANDRA MONAT

This small creature has a combination of stuffed and un-stuffed body parts. Unlike most of the toys in this book, only one of each body shape is cut out at the beginning; these are then sewn onto the remaining fabric before being cut out. This method is used because the pieces are small and the interlock fabric has a tendency to roll up at the edges, which can make sewing a bit fiddly.

FINISHED SIZE

- 14 cm × 12 cm (5½ in × 5 in) – body only

TOOLS

- Tracing paper
- Fabric marker
- Scissors
- Pins
- Sewing needle
- Sewing machine
- Stuffing stick (or chopstick)

MATERIALS

- Body fabric – a 40 cm × 60 cm (16 in × 24 in) piece of plain interlock fabric (this fabric is easy to turn right side out) or use an old sweatshirt or heavy T-shirt.
- Extra fabric – a scrap of contrasting cotton fabric for the inner ears; a scrap of patterned cotton fabric for the nose; a scrap of embroidery backing paper (tissue paper also works).
- Thread – coloured sewing thread to match body fabric and nose fabric; sewing thread or embroidery thread in a contrasting colour for the mouth and eyes.
- Stuffing – polyfill.

{CONTINUED}

INSTRUCTIONS

1 Trace and cut out the enlarged pattern using the template provided. Pin it to the appropriate fabric and cut out the pieces. At this stage, you only need to cut 1 body shape, 2 leg shapes, 2 arm shapes, 2 ear shapes, 2 inner ear shapes and 1 nose shape from your fabric. (You should have half the body fabric remaining for later use.)

2 Pin the embroidery backing paper onto the wrong side of the body fabric, behind where the face will be. Pin the nose shape right-side up on the right side of the body piece (as marked on the pattern). Use matching sewing thread to sew the nose to the body using a small, tight zigzag stitch.

3 Using embroidery thread, hand stitch a wavy line from one side of the face to the other (as marked on the pattern), or use a small, tight zigzag stitch on the sewing machine, sewing slowly and carefully. Using the same thread, embroider the eyes by hand (as marked on the pattern). Carefully tear away the backing paper.

4 Pin each inner ear piece onto an ear piece (as marked). Using sewing thread to match the body fabric, sew the inner ear pieces to the ears with a small, tight zigzag stitch.

5 Pin the ears onto the reserved body fabric (wrong sides facing), then sew around each using a small, tight zigzag stitch. Carefully cut around the ears, close to the sewing line, being careful not to clip the seam. You should now have 2 crinkled ears.

6 Pin the arm pieces to the reserved body fabric (right sides facing), then sew together using a small straight stitch, leaving the end of each arm open for turning right side out. With scissors, cut around each arm, leaving a seam allowance of 5 mm. Then trim all curves close to the stitch line, taking special care when clipping between the fingers. Turn arms right side out. Repeat this process to make the legs.

7 Place the body piece right side up on your work surface. Pin the ears and legs into position (x to x and y to y), pointing in towards the body and remembering which way they will face when the body is turned right side out. Pin the remaining body fabric to the body piece (right sides facing), making sure the legs and ears stay tucked inside. Sew around the body piece using a straight stitch, securing the ears and legs as you go, and remembering to leave an opening for turning right side out and stuffing (as marked on the pattern). After sewing, carefully cut around the body, leaving a seam allowance of 5 mm, then trim curves close to the stitch line. Turn right side out.

8 Using a stuffing stick, stuff the body firmly. Sew the stuffing opening closed using a whip stitch.

9 Sew the arm openings closed using a small whip stitch, then use a cross-stitch to attach them to the body (z to z).

{CONTINUED}

Template shown at 100% Seam allowance is included

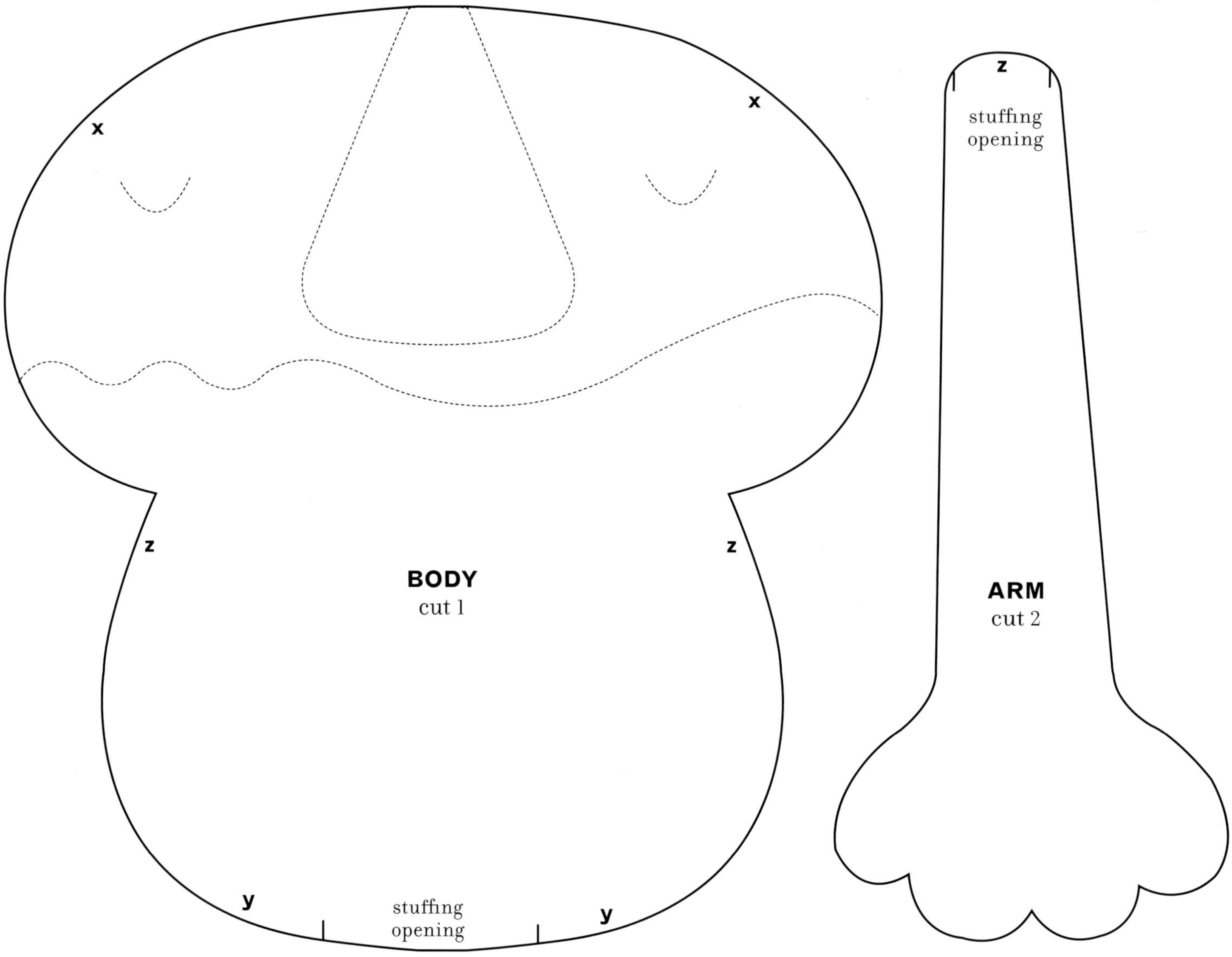

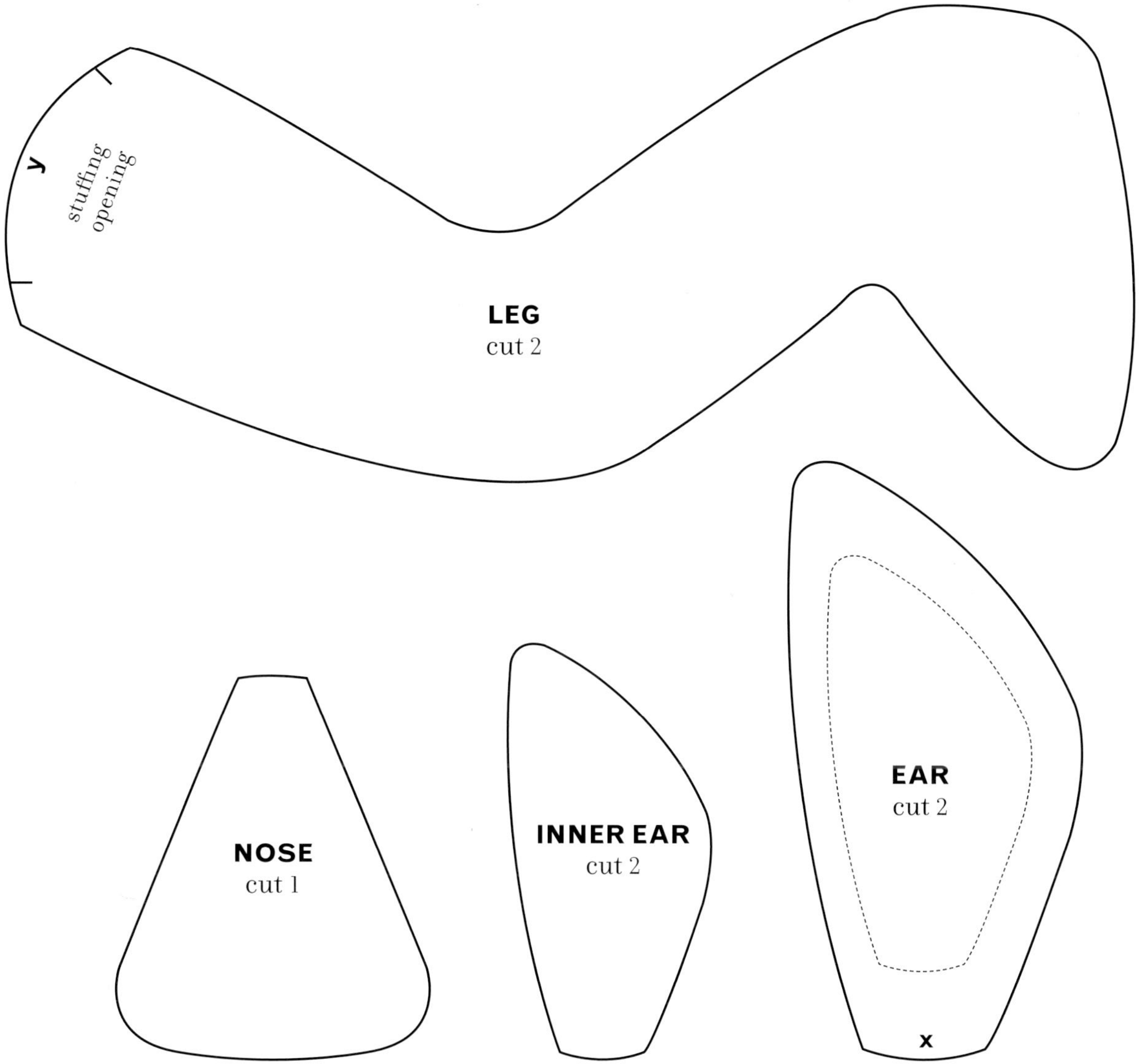
y
stuffing opening
LEG
cut 2
EAR
cut 2
x
NOSE
cut 1
INNER EAR
cut 2

pocket gnome

{Bonspiel Creation – www.bonspielcreation.com} ELLEN BOX

I came up with this idea when I was trying to make a garden gnome suitable for apartments and other indoor environments. This character provides lots of possibilities for surprises and sabotage – hide him in a pot plant or coat pocket, hang him in the shower, or squeeze him into someone's boot!

FINISHED SIZE

- 31 cm × 13 cm (12 in × 5 in)

TOOLS

- Tracing paper
- Fabric marker
- Scissors
- Pins
- Sewing needle
- Embroidery needle
- Sewing machine
- Craft glue
- Stuffing stick (or chopstick)

MATERIALS

- Body fabric – a 31 cm × 34 cm (12 in × 13 in) piece of good quality polar fleece, sweatshirt fleece, or other thick stretchy fabric.
- Extra fabric – scraps of felt for the face and eyes; a scrap of fake fur for the beard (or use real fur from an old fur coat).
- Thread – coloured sewing thread to match the body fabric, face felt and eyes; red embroidery thread for the mouth.
- Decorations – a 16 cm (6 in) length of 6–12 mm (¼–½ in) wide ribbon, for the hanging loop.
- Stuffing – polyfill, or cotton or wool rovings.

{CONTINUED}

{pocket gnome}

INSTRUCTIONS

1 Trace and cut out the enlarged pattern using the template provided. Pin it to the appropriate fabric and cut out the pieces. You will need to cut 2 body shapes, 1 face shape, 1 beard shape, 2 eye shapes and 2 pupil shapes from your fabric.

2 Use the craft glue to stick the pupils onto the eyes, then glue the eyes onto the face (as marked on the pattern). Set the sewing machine to a fairly short stitch length and sew around the pupils and eyes (or hand stitch them on). Using the embroidery needle, sew the mouth onto the face with embroidery thread (as marked).

3 Pin the face into position on one of the body pieces (as marked on the pattern), then machine or hand stitch on. Stitch the beard into place, securing it along the top edge only (this will allow the beard to flop over your pocket or over the edge of a teacup when gnome is in use).

4 Fold the length of ribbon in half and pin in place at the peak of the gnomes hat, with the length of the ribbon pointing in towards the body. Pin the 2 body pieces together (right sides facing) and sew, leaving an opening for turning right side out and stuffing (as marked). Turn right side out.

5 Using a stuffing stick, push small amounts of stuffing into the tight corners first – arms, legs and hat. Gradually fill the rest of the body until the stuffing is firm and even.

6 Sew the stuffing opening closed using a whip stitch.

{CONTINUED}

Enlarge template to 200% Seam allowance is included

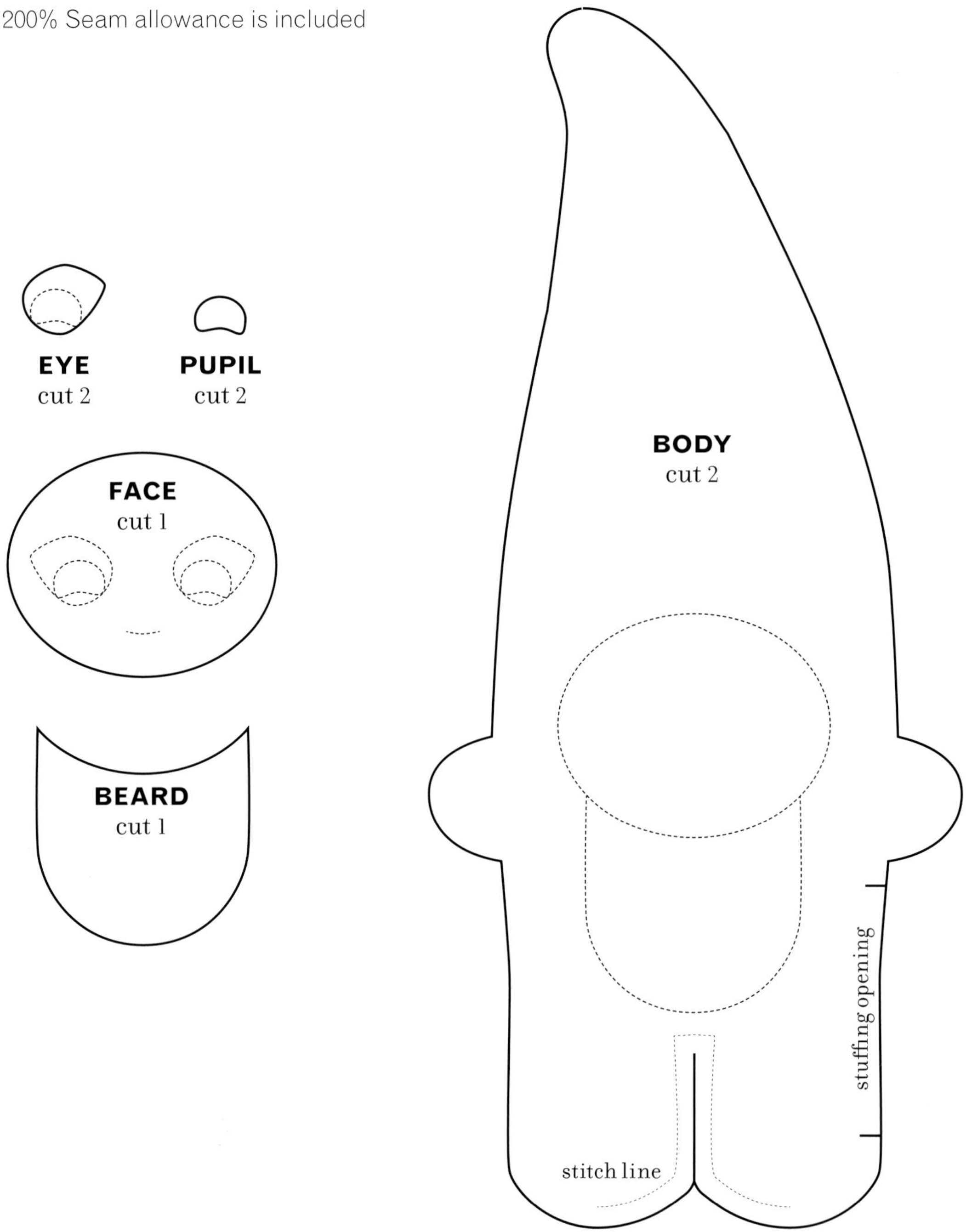

topsy-turvy tabitha

{Hatch – www.prairiemouse.typepad.com} LOUISE HATCHARD

Topsy-turvy Tabitha puts on her best dress and comes out to play, all day long. But when the stars are twinkling, she wears her soft nightgown and sleeps with sweet dreams, all night long.

FINISHED SIZE

- 25 cm × 10 cm (10 in × 4 in)

TOOLS

- Tracing paper
- Fabric marker
- Scissors
- Pins
- Sewing needle
- 9 cm (3½ in) doll needle
- Sewing machine
- Stuffing stick (or chopstick)
- Iron
- 30 cm (12 in) hardcover book

MATERIALS

- Body fabric – a 60 cm × 18 cm (24 in × 7 in) piece of patterned cotton fabric for the day skirt and a 12 cm × 6 cm (5 in × 2½ in) piece of the same fabric for the matching bodice; a 60 cm × 18 cm (24 in × 7 in) piece of patterned flannelette for the night skirt and a 12 cm × 6 cm (5 in × 2½ in) piece of the same fabric for the matching bodice; a 25 cm × 45 cm (10 in × 18 in) piece of linen or heavy cotton for the body and hands (iron a piece of light fusible interfacing onto the back if the fabric has a loose weave).
- Extra fabric – a 13 cm × 13 cm (5 in × 5 in) piece of fusible web; small scraps of white felt for the eyes and dress collar; a small piece of dark-grey or brown felt for the pupils.
- Thread – coloured sewing thread to match fabric; strong linen thread or crochet cotton to attach the skirt; embroidery thread in pink, dark-grey or brown, and pale-blue or green, for the face details.
- Decorations – a 30 cm (12 in) length of bias binding for the dress sash; a 30 cm (12 in) length of ribbon for the nightgown; a small vintage button for the dress collar; an 18 cm (7 in) length of cotton lace for the neck of the nightgown.
- Yarn – 25 g of brown 8-ply yarn, for the hair.
- Stuffing – polyfill.

{CONTINUED}

INSTRUCTIONS

1 Trace and cut out the enlarged pattern using the template provided. Pin it to the appropriate fabric and cut out the pieces. You will need to cut 2 body shapes, 8 hand shapes, 8 sleeve shapes (4 in each of the patterned fabrics); 2 of each bodice shape (1 set in each of the patterned fabrics); 1 of each collar shape; 2 eye shapes and 2 pupils from your fabric.

2 Sew the white felt eyes to one of the body pieces using tiny whip stitches (as marked on the pattern), then sew on the pupils. (I like to attach the eyes with fusible web first, to hold them in place while I sew.) With 3 strands of pink embroidery thread, embroider the noses on both faces using stem stitch, then embroider the 'awake' mouth. Embroider the 'sleeping' mouth using satin stitch. Embroider the sleeping eyes with 3 strands of the dark-grey thread using stem stitch.

3 Iron the fusible web to the wrong side of the 4 bodice pieces. Iron the 2 front bodice pieces to the front body piece, and the 2 back bodice pieces to the back body piece (the bodices will overlap slightly).

4 Use fusible web to attach the front felt collar piece to the front daydress bodice piece, then blanket stitch around the curved edge of the collar with blue or green embroidery thread. Use white sewing thread and tiny whip stitches to stitch around the straight edge. Repeat for the back collar piece. Sew on the decorative button in the centre of the front collar (see photo on page 66).

5 Cut the length of cotton lace in half and machine stitch to the neckline of the nightgown bodice on the front and back.

6 For each arm, sew one sleeve shape to a hand shape (right sides facing), x to x, then iron the seams flat. Pin 2 matching arm pieces together (right sides facing), and sew, leaving a small opening for turning right side out and stuffing (as marked on the pattern). Turn each arm right side out and iron.

7 Place the front body piece right side up on your work surface. Place the arms in position (y to y), pointing in towards the body. Baste in place. Place the back body piece right side down on top and baste the 2 body

{CONTINUED}

pieces together, making sure the arms stay tucked inside. Sew around the body, securing the limbs in place as you go, and leaving an opening for turning right side out and stuffing (as marked). Turn body right side out.

8 Using a stuffing stick, stuff each arm firmly. Sew the stuffing openings closed using a very small whip stitch. Stuff the body quite firmly and sew the opening closed using a whip stitch.

9 To make the hair, wind the brown yarn around the hardcover book 20 times, not too tightly (use a taller book if you would like the hair longer). Carefully remove from the book and hand stitch across the middle, to make the part in the hair – the part should measure about 3 cm (1 in) across. Repeat to make a second wig.

10 Secure the hair to the heads, stitching the part of each wig to the centre of the head. Cut the end loops. Make bunches from the hair on the awake doll and plaits for the sleeping doll (as shown in the photographs). For each, sew the hair to either side of the head (at z) with small stitches. Tie some ribbon around the bunches, and some embroidery thread around the end of the plaits.

11 For each skirt, fold the skirt fabric in half so the short edges meet (right sides facing), and sew down the short edge. Iron this seam flat. Put one skirt inside the other (right sides facing) and match up the seams. Pin the bottom edges together, then machine sew all the way around. Open this piece out and press the seam flat. Then fold the piece so that the wrong sides are facing and iron around the sewn seam so it sits nice and flat. Pin the 2 fabrics together around the raw edge and then sew using an overlocker or with a zigzag stitch.

12 Thread a needle with a piece of strong linen thread or a piece of crochet cotton doubled. Stitch around the top edge of the skirt (the edge you've just sewn) using a running stitch. Gently pull the threads to gather up the skirt, then place it around the doll's middle, making sure it is the right way up, so the skirt fabric matches the bodice fabric (it doesn't matter if you sew on the daydress or nightgown side of the skirt).

{CONTINUED}

Pull the skirt tight so it fits snugly around the doll, and position it so you can't see the non-matching bodice fabric. Sew the skirt to the doll, catching the skirt and then the bodice of the doll with your thread (you may need to go around twice to make sure it is firm and secure).

13 For the nightgown, position the ribbon over the gathered edge of the skirt and sew on, using tiny stitches along the top and bottom edges of the sash (start and end in the middle of the front of the doll). Tie the ribbon in a bow at the front. Repeat for the daydress with the bias binding, but start and end in the middle of the back and tie the bow there. When you are sewing, be careful that your stitches don't go right through the skirt fabric and catch the doll underneath.

Enlarge template to 200% Seam allowance is included

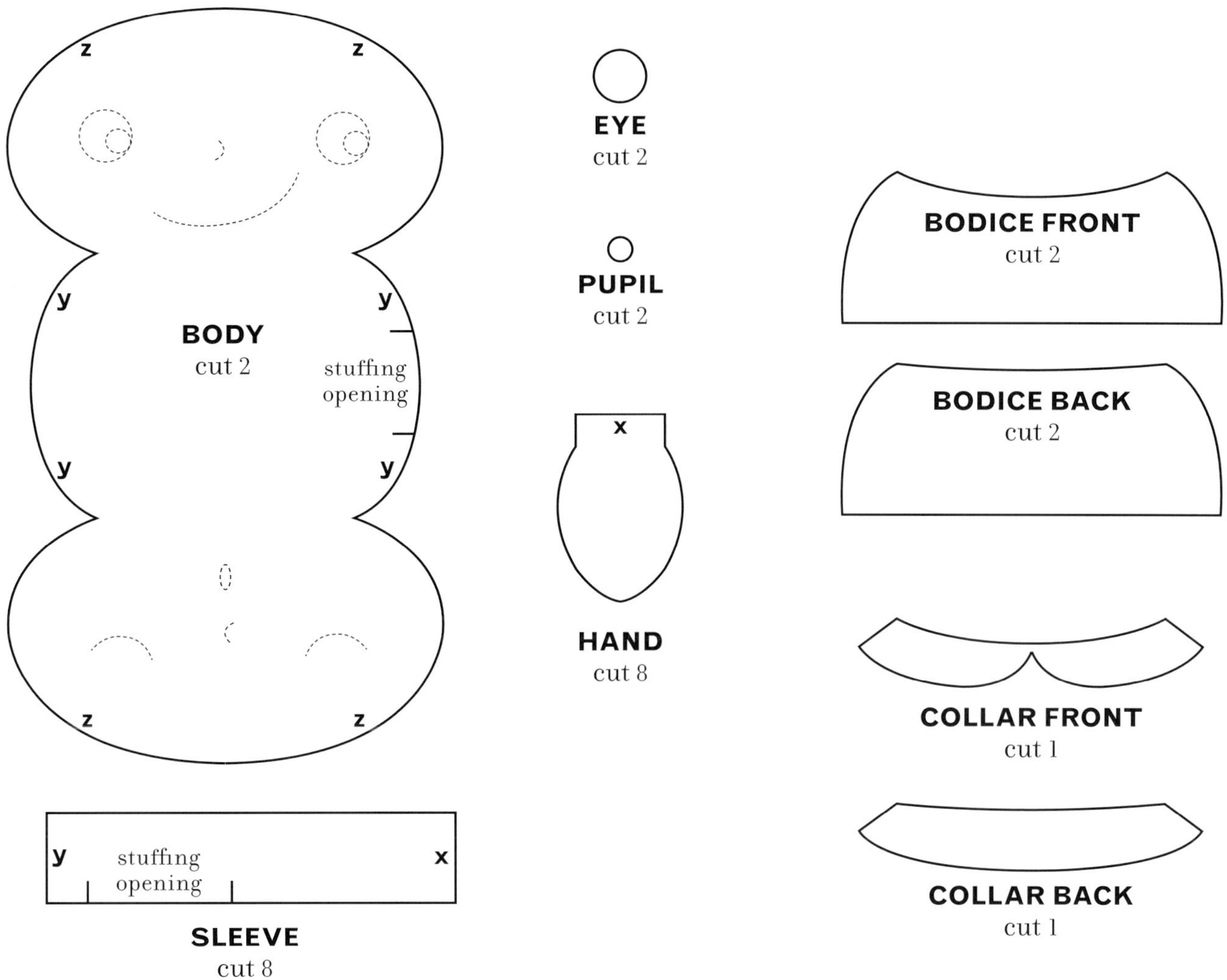

robot bear

{H. Luv Fabrications – mciverson.com} HEIDI IVERSON

Robot bear and I hang out and knit together (in the photo he's wearing the first scarf he ever knitted). We also drink tea and read crime novels – we're big fans of Raymond Chandler.

FINISHED SIZE

- 50 cm × 18 cm (20 in × 7 in)

TOOLS

- Tracing paper
- Fabric marker
- Scissors
- Pinking shears
- Pins
- Sewing needles
- Tapestry needle
- Sewing machine
- 2 × 3.25 mm (US size 3/UK size 10) knitting needles
- Stuffing stick (or chopstick)

MATERIALS

- Body fabric – a 54 cm × 36 cm (21 in × 14 in) piece of felt for the body and ears.
- Extra fabric – a 13 cm × 8 cm (5 in × 3 in) piece of fabric for the face mask (I used a vintage necktie); scraps of felt for the eyes; a 51 cm × 26 cm (20 in × 10 in) piece of muslin or felt for the arms.
- Thread – sewing thread in 4 different colours: one colour to match the body fabric, one colour to match the arm fabric, and 2 contrasting colours. A small amount of pearl cotton, embroidery thread or fingering-weight yarn, for embroidering the mouth.
- Yarn – 37 metres (40 yards) fingering-weight yarn, for the scarf.
- Stuffing – polyfill.

{CONTINUED}

{robot bear}

INSTRUCTIONS

1 Trace and cut out the enlarged pattern using the template provided. Pin it to the appropriate fabric and cut out the pieces. You will need to cut 2 body shapes, 1 face mask shape, 2 eye shapes, 2 ear shapes and 4 arm shapes from your fabric. Use scissors to cut out the face mask, arms and eyes and use pinking shears to cut out the body and ears.

2 Pin the face mask right side up to one of the body pieces (as marked on the pattern). Set the sewing machine to satin stitch and use a contrasting thread colour to stitch the face mask onto the head.

3 Pin the eyes onto the face mask (as marked). Using a different coloured contrasting thread, satin-stitch the eyes onto the face mask.

4 With the tapestry needle, use pearl cotton, embroidery thread or fingering-weight yarn to embroider the mouth using single straight stitches (as marked on the pattern).

5 For each arm, pin 2 pieces together (right sides facing), then sew, leaving the straight edge open for turning right side out and stuffing. Turn right side out. Use a stuffing stick to stuff the arms firmly.

6 Place the front body piece wrong side up on your work surface. Fold and pin-tuck the ears, then pin them into position on the body (x to x). Pin the arms onto the body (y to y). Place the second body piece wrong side down on top and pin the 2 body pieces together. Sew, using a straight stitch on the machine, securing the limbs and ears in place as you go, and leaving an opening for stuffing (as marked).

7 Using a stuffing stick, push small amounts of stuffing into the legs and head first. Then gradually fill the body until the stuffing is firm and even. Sew the stuffing opening closed using a straight stitch, either by hand or using the sewing machine.

8 The final step is to knit the scarf. Using the fingering-weight yarn, cast 10 stitches onto your knitting needles. Knit every stitch and every row, until the scarf is 30 cm (12 in) long (or as long as you like). Bind all of the stitches, then add a fringe to each end. To make the fringes, cut twenty 14 cm (5½ in) lengths of the yarn, then fold each length in half. To attach each length to the edge of the scarf, use a crochet hook to pull the loop through a hole in the knit, then feed the ends of the yarn through the loop and pull tight to secure. Attach ten lengths evenly along each end of the scarf. Wrap the scarf around Robot Bear's neck.

{CONTINUED}

Enlarge template to 200% Seam allowance is included

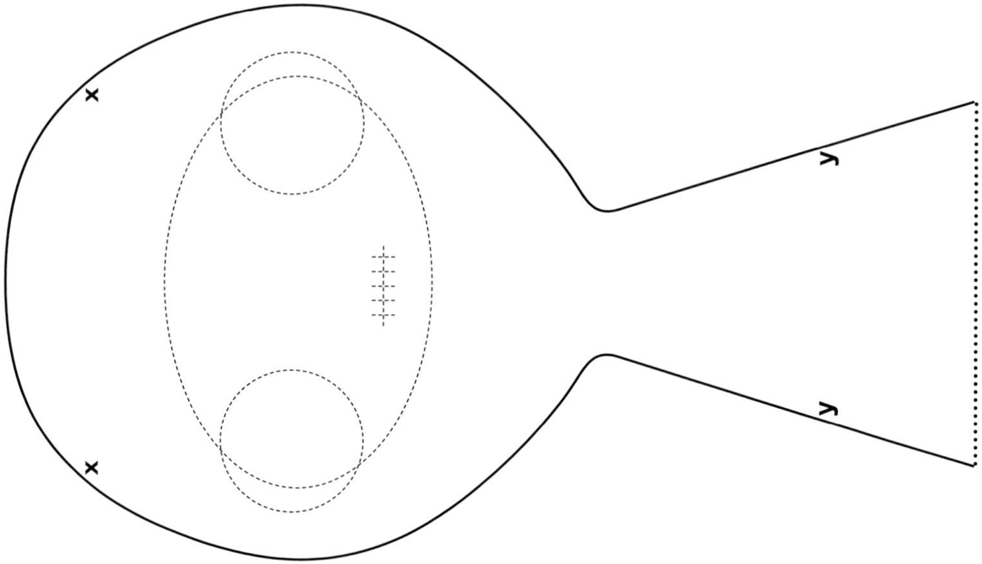

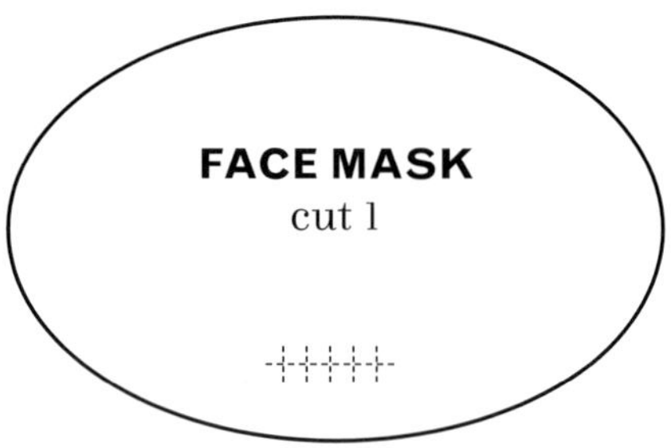

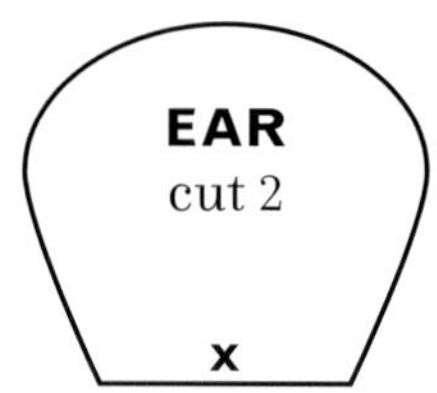

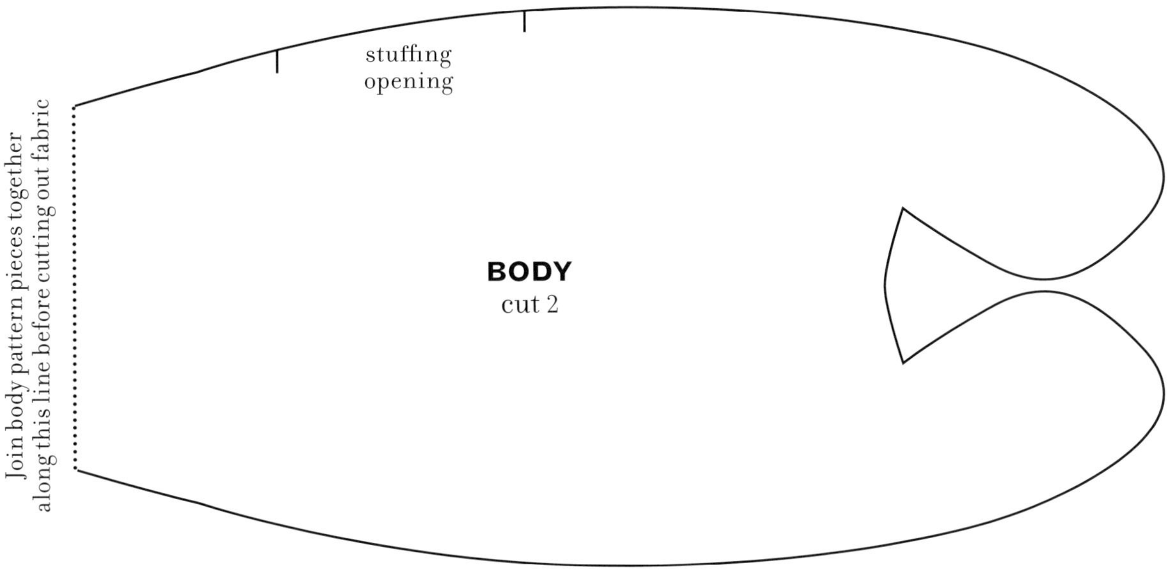
Join body pattern pieces together
along this line before cutting out fabric
stuffing
opening
BODY
cut 2

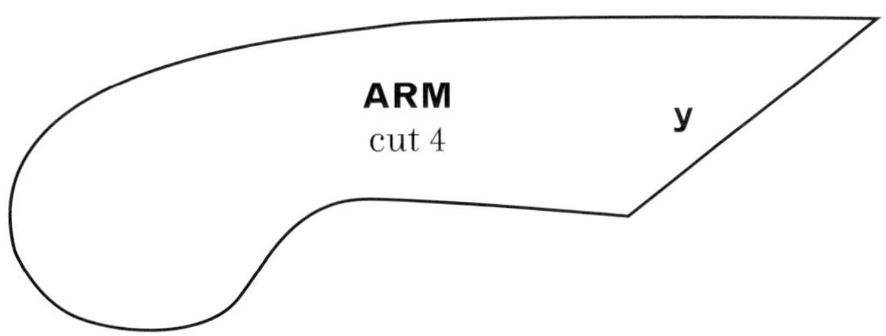
ARM
cut 4
y

little pup

{My Little Mochi – www.mylittlemochi.typepad.com} MYRA MASUDA

I've always been drawn to antique toys, especially those that show signs of having had a lot of love. This dog toy was made for my son, inspired by the stuffed animal carnival prizes I loved as a child. Little Pup may be small in size but he gives back lots of love and is the perfect size for your pocket.

FINISHED SIZE

- 11.5 cm × 6.5 cm (4½ in × 2½ in)

TOOLS

- Tracing paper
- Fabric marker
- Scissors
- Pins
- Sewing needle
- Doll needle
- Sewing machine
- Stuffing stick (or chopstick)
- Iron

MATERIALS

- Body fabric – a 25 cm × 25 cm (10 in × 10 in) piece of plain lightweight fabric, such as linen or 100 per cent cotton.
- Extra fabric – a 20 cm × 15 cm (8 in × 6 in) piece of patterned fabric for the ears, inner arms and gusset; a scrap of white felt for the eyes and a scrap of black felt for the nose.
- Thread – coloured sewing thread to match body fabric; extra-strong thread, such as quilting thread, for attaching the arms; white, black and pink embroidery thread for the face details.
- Stuffing – polyfill and plastic pellets.
- Decorations – two black 11 mm (⅖ in) buttons for eyes; two clear 9.5 mm (⅓ in) buttons for securing the arms.

{CONTINUED}

{little pup}

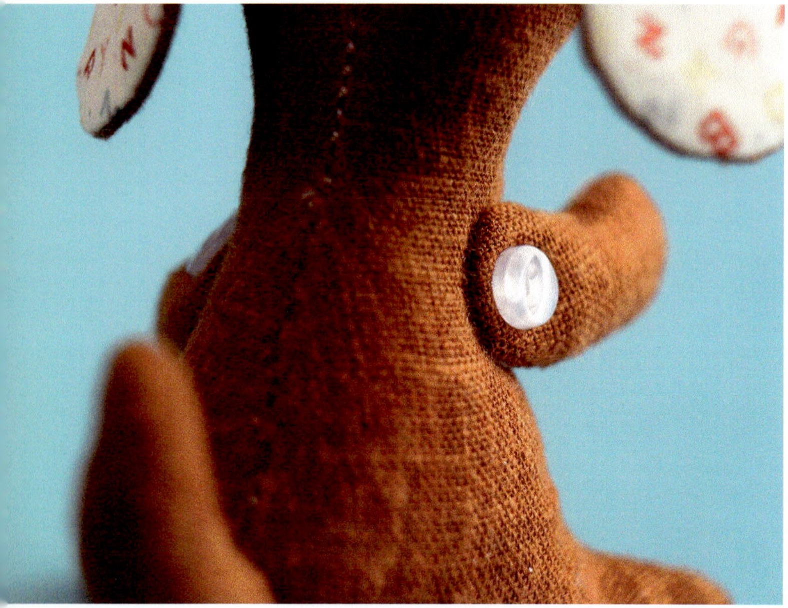

INSTRUCTIONS

1 Trace and cut out the pattern using the template provided. Pin it to the appropriate fabric and cut out the pieces. You will need to cut 2 main body shapes, 1 inner body shape, 1 gusset shape, 4 arm shapes (2 in plain fabric and 2 in patterned fabric), 4 ear shapes (2 in plain fabric and 2 in patterned fabric), 1 nose shape and 2 eye shapes from your fabric.

2 For each arm, pin together a solid-colour piece and a patterned piece (right sides facing), and sew, leaving an opening for turning right side out and stuffing (as marked on the pattern). Trim around the stitch line, leaving a 3 mm (⅛ in) seam allowance. Repeat for each ear, leaving the straight edge open for turning right side out. Turn arms and ears right side out and iron.

3 Position an ear on the right side of each main body piece, patterned side facing up (as marked on the pattern). Baste into place, with the straight edge of the ear about 3 mm (⅛ in) from the edge of the head (as marked on the pattern).

4 Pin main body pieces together (right sides facing). Baste the gusset piece to each body piece, C to C and E to E. Sew from C to E, securing the ears as you go. Then sew the 2 body pieces together, sewing from C to A around the nose, and from E to B down the back, leaving an opening for turning right side out and stuffing (as marked). (I like to keep the ears out of the way during sewing by folding the ears toward the nose of the dog and basting them in place with a couple of stitches. Remove the stitches from the ears after you finish sewing the main body pieces together.)

5 Pin the inner body piece to the main body, A to A and B to B, (right sides facing). Baste from A to B on both sides of the inner body piece, then sew. Turn the dog right side out.

6 Place some plastic pellets into the base of the body and legs and then stuff the body firmly with polyfill. Sew the stuffing opening closed using ladder stitch.

7 Use a small blanket stitch and white embroidery thread to attach the white felt eyes to the face (as marked on the pattern). Then use black embroidery thread to sew a black button onto each eye. With pink embroidery thread, use a back stitch to embroider the mouth onto the face (as marked on the pattern).

8 To make the nose, sew a running stitch around the edge of the black felt round. Place a pinch of stuffing in the centre, then carefully gather the thread, tucking the edges of the felt inside, to create a ball. Sew to secure. Baste the nose onto the dog's snout at C, then sew in place.

9 Using a stuffing stick, stuff the arms firmly. Sew the stuffing openings closed using a small ladder stitch.

10 To attach the arms to the body, thread a doll needle with a 50 cm (20 in) length of extra-strong sewing thread. Double the thread over (so you're sewing with a double-thickness) and tie a knot at the end. Insert the needle into the patterned side of one of the arms (at x), come out through the front of the arm and then pass the needle through a hole in a clear button. Pass the needle back through the second hole in the button

{CONTINUED}

and back through the arm. Then insert the needle into the body (at x), coming out on the opposite side of the body. Push the needle through the other arm from the patterned side (at x), through the second clear button, back through the button and arm and through the body, coming out on the other side, under the first arm you secured. Pull the thread tight so arms sit snugly against the body. Wind the thread around the thread joining the arm to the body piece, then tie a knot to secure. Hide the thread in the body by inserting the needle back into the body near x, coming out on the other side of the body, then cutting the thread close to the body.

11 Pin the tail pieces together (right sides facing), then sew, leaving the base open for turning right side out. Trim around the stitch line, leaving a 3 mm (⅛ in) seam allowance. Turn right side out and stuff. Loosely sew the stuffing opening closed using a ladder stitch, then baste the tail onto the body at D. Sew the tail on using a small ladder stitch.

Template shown at 100% Seam allowance is included

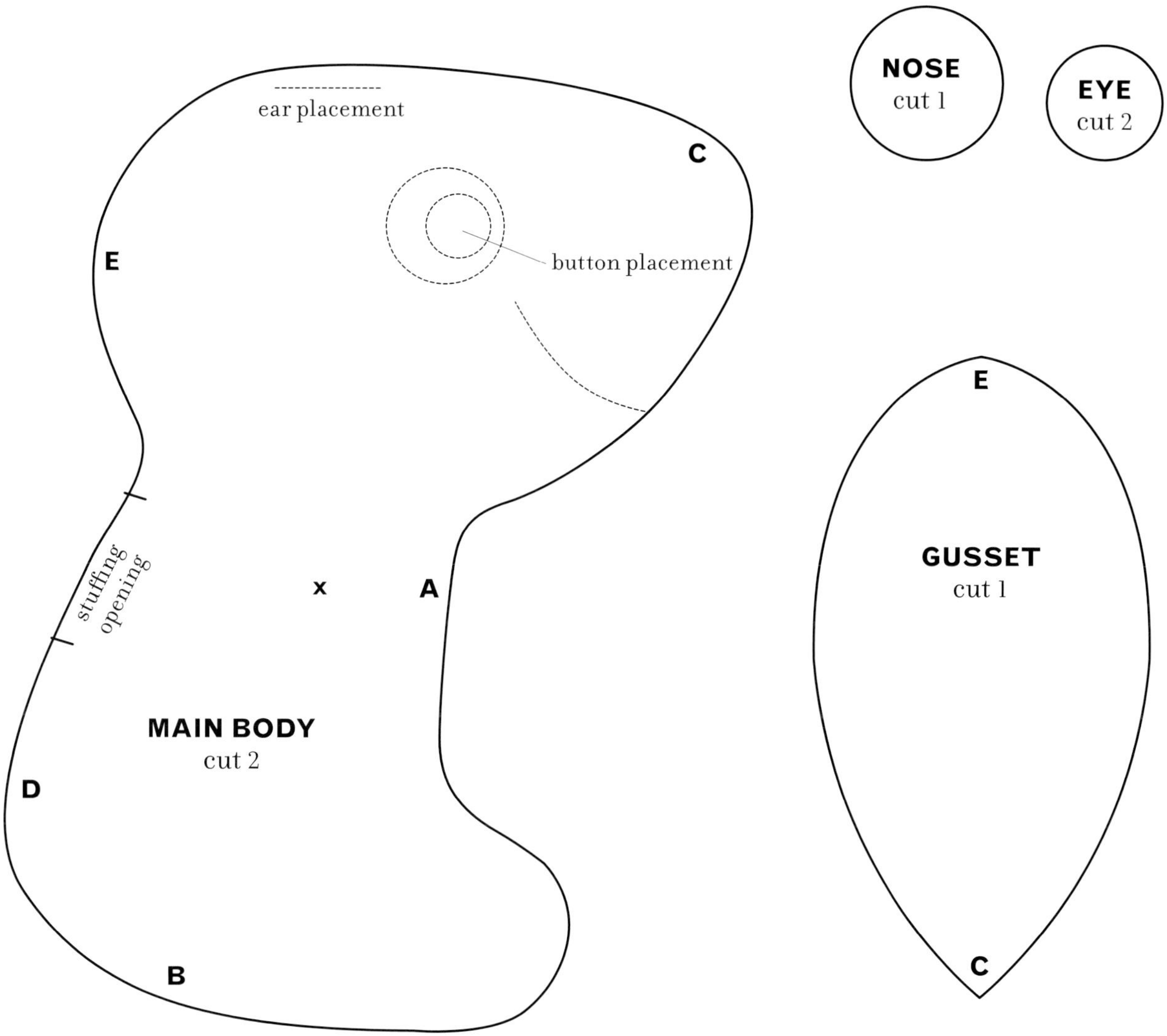

(CONTINUED)

Template shown at 100% Seam allowance is included

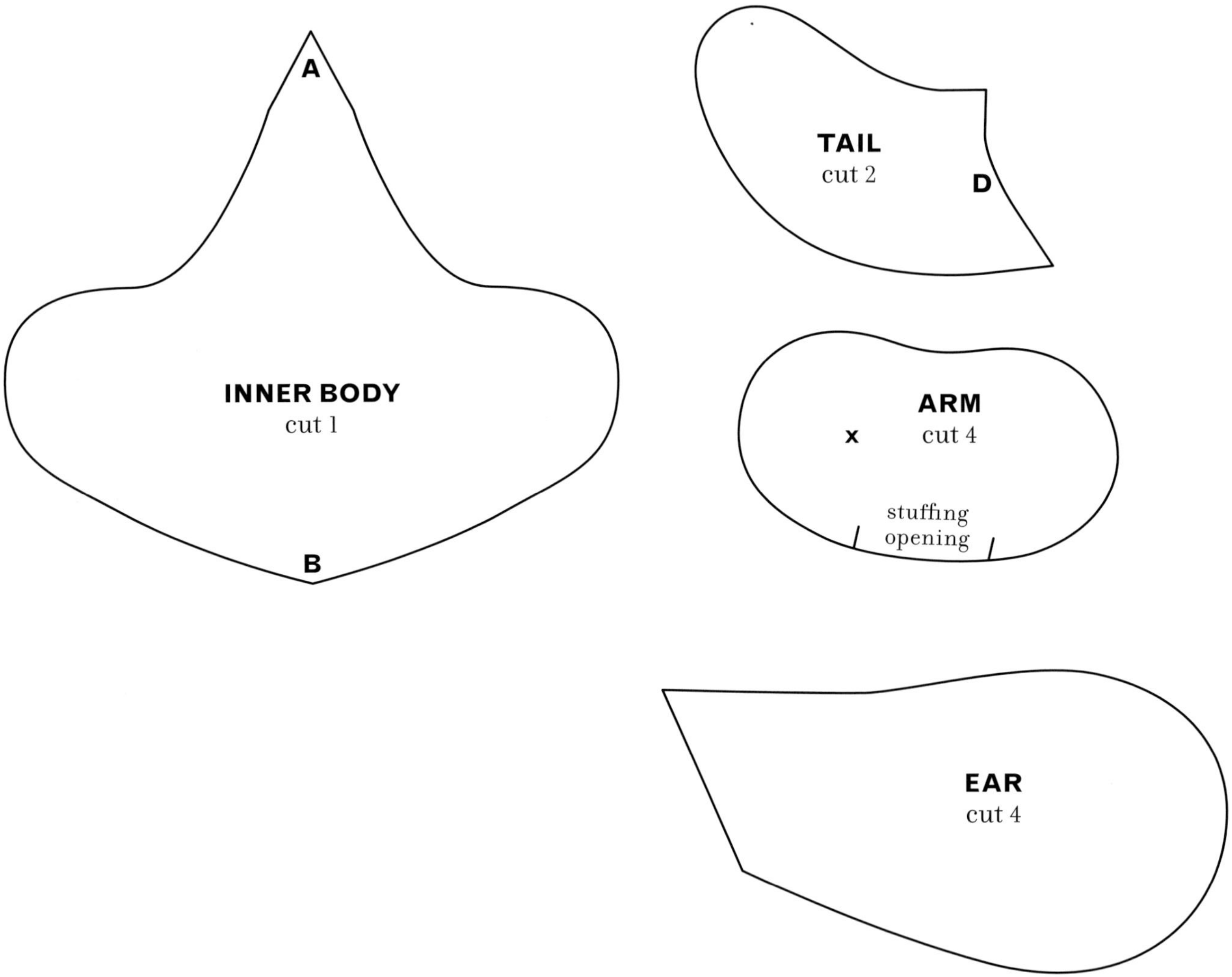

patchwork horse

{While She Naps – www.whileshenaps.typepad.com} ABIGAIL PATNER GLASSENBERG

This patchwork horse has the look of an old-fashioned, classic stuffed toy and would make a charming addition to a baby's nursery. Use vintage prints and buttons to give it even more of an heirloom feel.

FINISHED SIZE

- 20 cm × 25 cm (8 in × 10 in)

TOOLS

- Tracing paper (I use freezer paper because you can iron it to the fabric so you don't need to pin)
- Fabric marking pen
- Scissors
- Pins
- Sewing needle
- 13 cm (5 in) doll needle
- Sewing machine
- Stuffing stick (I use surgical forceps)
- Iron

MATERIALS

- Body fabric – a 30 cm × 36 cm (12 in × 14 in) piece of patterned cotton fabric, or about seven 5 cm × 30 cm (2 in × 12 in) strips of 4 or 5 different fabrics to make patchwork, for the body and head gusset.
- Extra fabric – a 30 cm × 30 cm (12 in × 12 in) piece of plain cotton fabric for the legs, footpads, tail and mane.
- Thread – coloured sewing thread to match fabric; extra-strong sewing thread for attaching the legs.
- Stuffing – polyfill.
- Decorations – four matching buttons, for attaching the legs.
- A 5 cm × 11.5 cm (2 in × 4½ in) piece of sturdy cardboard.

{CONTINUED}

INSTRUCTIONS

1 If you choose to use patchwork for the body fabric, use a very short stitch length on your sewing machine to sew the fabric strips to each other (right sides facing), one at a time, to create a piece of patchwork measuring about 30 cm x 36 cm (12 in x 14 in). Iron all seams flat.

2 Trace and cut out the enlarged pattern using the template provided. Pin (or iron) it to the appropriate fabric and cut out the pieces. You will need to cut 2 body shapes, 4 ear shapes, 4 foot pad shapes, 4 rear leg shapes, 4 front leg shapes and 1 gusset shape from your fabric.

3 Pin one of the body pieces to the gusset piece, A to A and B to B, (right sides facing). Sew from A to B. Pin the second body piece to the other side of the gusset piece (body pieces right sides facing), A to A and B to B. Sew from A to B. Sew the rest of the way around the body, leaving an opening for turning inside out and stuffing (as marked on the pattern). Turn the body right side out.

4 Using a stuffing stick, push small amounts of stuffing into the body, starting with the nose and then gradually filling the rest of the body until it is firm and even. Sew the stuffing opening closed using a ladder stitch (this seam will be hidden by the tail on the finished toy).

5 For each of the ears, pin 2 ear shapes together (right sides facing) and sew, leaving the straight edge open for turning right side out. Turn right side out. Turn the raw edge under 3 mm (⅛ in) and iron flat. Close the opening with a neat ladder stitch. Pin the ears to the body (as marked on the pattern) and sew on using a neat ladder stitch.

6 For each rear leg, pin 2 rear leg shapes together (right sides facing), and sew, leaving the straight edge open and leaving an opening for turning right side out and stuffing (as marked on the pattern). Repeat for front legs.

7 For each leg, insert a footpad shape into the straight edge of the leg and pin. Using a tiny, firm back stitch, sew the footpad in place. Turn legs right side out.

{CONTINUED}

8 Use a stuffing stick to stuff each leg firmly with polyfill. Sew stuffing openings closed using a neat ladder stitch.

9 To attach the legs to the body, thread the doll needle with extra-strong sewing thread. For the rear legs, insert the needle through the back of one leg (at x), come out through the front of the leg and then pass the needle through a hole in a decorative button. Pass the needle back through the second hole in the button and through the leg. Then insert the needle into the body (at x), coming out on the opposite side of the body. Push the needle through the other back leg, through a decorative button and back through the button and leg. Push the needle back through the body and through each leg and button 2 or 3 more times, pulling the thread taught each time, until the legs are firmly attached. Tie off the thread with a double knot underneath one of the legs so that the stray threads are hidden. Repeat (at y) for the front legs.

10 Tear or cut lots of long strips from the remaining plain fabric. To make the tail, wrap the strips around the short edges of the piece of cardboard. When one strip ends just hold another strip down on top of it and continue until the cardboard is fairly well covered. Carefully remove the fabric strips from the cardboard and wrap a strip of fabric around one end, about 15 mm (½ in) from the base, and tie a knot to secure. Use scissors to cut the loops at the other end of the tail. Pin the tail onto the body at z, then sew it on with extra-strong sewing thread, using a ladder stitch.

11 To make the mane, cut a slit lengthways down the centre of the cardboard, nearly to the end. Wrap long strips of fabric around the long edges of the cardboard, from the cut end all the way along to where the slit finishes. Once the cardboard is fairly well covered, use the sewing machine to sew down the centre (along the slit), to attach all the strips together. Slide the fabric off the cardboard and cut through the ends of the loops on either side. Pin the mane to the body (stretching from C to D) and sew into place with extra-strong sewing thread, using a ladder stitch.

{CONTINUED}

Enlarge template to 200% Seam allowance is included

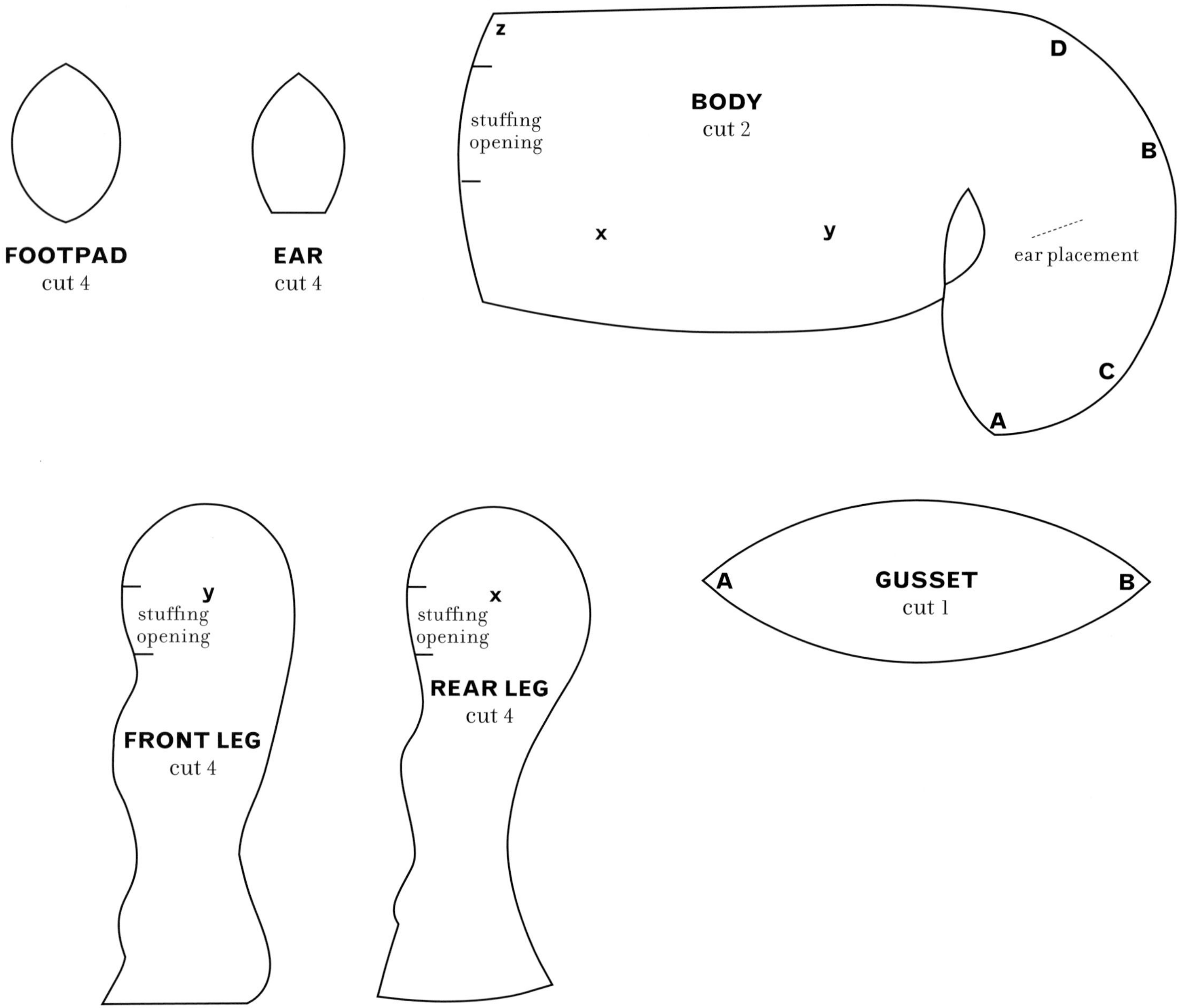

sgt. pepper's turtles

{Electric Sheep Fiber Arts – amysbabies.etsy.com} AMY J SHIMEL

My father is a huge Beatles fan. When I was growing up, we listened to their albums together and so I became a big Beatles fan too. When I started designing amigurumi dolls, I wanted to make toys that were challenging and would represent the things that I love the most. I chose to make the Sgt. Pepper's Lonely Hearts Club Turtles as homage to one of the Beatles' most iconic album covers. (This is an easy crochet pattern, but it is intensive in terms of detail.)

FINISHED SIZE

- Each: 8 cm (3 in) × 6 cm (2 in)

TOOLS

- Crochet hook: 1 × 3.5 mm (size E/4)
- Steel hook: 1 × 1.8 mm (size 6)
- Tapestry needle
- Sewing needle

MATERIALS

- YARN
  White: 50 metres (55 yards) – heads and feet.
  Bright-yellow: 18 metres (20 yards) – John's shell.
  Bright-blue: 18 metres (20 yards) – Paul's shell.
  Bright-red: 18 metres (20 yards) – George's shell.
  Bright-pink: 18 metres (20 yards) – Ringo's shell.
  Bright-green: 8 cm (3 in) – feather in George's hat.
- **THREAD** – white sewing thread; 5 skeins black embroidery thread for the hair and moustaches.
- **DECORATIONS** – 6 black beads size 6/0 E (3.3 mm) for eyes; 40 gold beads size 10/0 (2 mm) for uniform buttons.
- **STUFFING** – plastic pellets and a small amount of polyfill.

ABBREVIATIONS

- **ch** chain
- **sl st** slip stitch
- **dc** double crochet (**sc** single crochet in the US)
- **tr** treble crochet (**dc** double crochet US)
- **dc dec** decrease 1 stitch with double crochet (**sc dec** or **sc 2tog** decrease 1 stitch with single crochet in the US)
- ***** indicates beginning of a section to be repeated

{CONTINUED}

NOTES

The dolls are worked in the round. Mark the last stitch in each round to keep track of where you are supposed to stop each round. These dolls are crocheted with a very tight tension (gauge) – tension is 6 stitches and 6 rows per 2.5 cm (1 in). Tight tension will stop the stuffing from showing through the stitches and help the dolls keep their shape. Work through both loops unless instructed otherwise.

There are several places in this pattern where you will be required to split the yarn and use only 2 ply instead of the standard 4 ply.

Some parts of these dolls are started using a self-tightening ring (see instructions on pages 36–37).

INSTRUCTIONS

For reference: John has the yellow shell, Paul has the blue, George has the red, and Ringo has the pink.

1 SHELLS

Make 1 in each shell colour:

R1 6 dc into the ring and pull the ring tight. Mark the last stitch. (6 dc.)

R2 2 dc into each stitch around. (12 dc.)

R3 *1 dc, 2 dc into next stitch, repeat from * 5 more times. (18 dc.)

R4 *2 dc, 2 dc into next stitch, repeat from * 5 more times. (24 dc.)

R5 *3 dc, 2 dc into next stitch, repeat from * 5 more times. (30 dc.)

R6 *4 dc, 2 dc into next stitch, repeat from * 5 more times. (36 dc.)

R7–11 dc into each stitch around. (36 dc.)

Finish off and leave a tail long enough to use to sew the shells and bellies together.

{CONTINUED}

2 BELLIES

Make 1 in each shell colour:

R1 6 dc into the ring and pull the ring tight. Mark the last stitch. (6 dc.)
R2 2 dc into each stitch around. (12 dc.)
R3 *1 dc, 2 dc into next stitch, repeat from * 5 more times. (18 dc.)
R4 *2 dc, 2 dc into next stitch, repeat from * 5 more times. (24 dc.)
R5 *3 dc, 2 dc into next stitch, repeat from * 5 more times. (30 dc.)
R6 *4 dc, 2 dc into next stitch, repeat from * 5 more times. (36 dc.)

Finish off.

3 FEET

With white yarn (make 16):

R1 6 dc into the ring and pull the ring tight. Mark the last stitch. (6 dc.)
R2 2 dc into each stitch around. (12 dc.)
R3 dc into each stitch around. (12 dc)
R4 *dc into next 4 stitches, dc dec, repeat from * once. (10 dc.)

Finish off and pinch each flat.

4 HEADS

With white yarn (make 4):

R1 6 dc into the ring and pull the ring tight. Mark the last stitch. (6 dc.)
R2 2 dc into each stitch around. (12 dc.)
R3 *1 dc, 2 dc into next stitch, repeat from * 5 more times. (18 dc.)
R4 *2 dc, 2 dc into next stitch, repeat from * 5 more times. (24 dc.)
R5–7 dc into each stitch around. (24 dc.)
R8 *2 dc, dc dec, repeat from * 5 more times. (18 dc.)
R9 *1 dc, dc dec, repeat from * 5 more times. (12 dc.)
R10–12 dc into each stitch around. (12 dc.)

Switch to a shell colour:

R13 dc into each stitch around. (12 dc.)
R14 In *back loops only*, dc into each stitch around. (12 dc.)

In all other rows: working in both loops, continue to dc into all stitches around until the neck measures 6 cm (2½ in) long from the bottom of the head.

Go back to the place where you worked in the back loops only. In the centre front of the neck, using the shell colour, ch 3 into the first loop and work a tr into each missed loop around. Ch 2 and sl st into last stitch. The gap is the opening in the front of the standing uniform collar.

Finish off.

5 Stuff each head firmly with a small amount of polyfill. Push the polyfill more towards the gap in the collar to create a rounded shape where the front of the head and face area will be.

6 Using white sewing thread and the sewing needle, sew 2 black bead eyes onto each of the heads, except for John's (as shown in the photograph). On John's head, use black embroidery thread to make French knots for eyes, then sew sleepy eyelids and large round glasses.

7 Thread the tapestry needle with white yarn and use to make a nose on Ringo's face: start by making 2 or 3 vertical stitches where you want the bottom of the nose to be, then make every stitch after that start a little bit higher on his face, but end in the same place at the bottom. Make the nose narrower as you work up the face. This will build up the nose.

8 Using the black embroidery thread, use straight stitches to give each head a groovy moustache.

9 UNIFORM DETAILS

The uniforms are decorated with contrasting yarn. For John (yellow shell) use red yarn; for Paul (blue shell) and George (red shell) use white yarn; and for Ringo (pink shell) use yellow yarn.

Using 2 strands of the contrasting yarn and the sewing needle:
Sew a line of stem stitch up the centre of the neck to the collar opening. Sew up one side of the collar, around, and back down the centre line. Then make 5 horizontal lines on each side of the centre line.

{CONTINUED}

Using the white sewing thread, attach a gold bead at each end of the 5 horizontal lines (10 beads total for each turtle).

10 Using the tapestry needle and the tail left on the shell, begin assembling each turtle. The easiest way is to match up the natural holes in the crochet and use a running stitch: sandwich each foot between the shell and the belly and sew through all 3 pieces. Sew 2 feet, then attach the head, then sew on the other 2 feet, making 2 or 3 stitches between each body part, to secure the belly to the body. When you are almost back to where you started, fill the body with plastic pellets, then sew the last few stitches to close the opening. Finish off with a knot and hide the knot inside the body by popping it through the nearest crochet hole. *But do not cut the yarn yet.*

11 Bend the neck up and position the head where you want it to rest on the body. Push the needle through the body until it comes out around the bottom of the collar. Push the needle through the neck and back into the shell. This stitch will hold the head in position. Finish off, hide the knot in the body and cut off the yarn.

12 Using the contrasting colour again, sew a line of stem stitch around the bottom of each shell.

13 FINAL UNIFORM DETAILS

Each turtle has a cord on his right shoulder. For John and Paul use red yarn to make the cord; for George use white yarn; and for Ringo use blue yarn.

Using the steel hook and 2 strands of the appropriate yarn, crochet a chain about 10 cm (4 in) long. Leave a tail on each end long enough to be pulled inside the body with the crochet hook.

To attach the cord to the shoulder, use the white sewing thread and sewing needle along with the steel crochet hook: use the crochet hook to pop the knotted end of the chain into the body just below the bottom horizontal stripe. Line the cord up vertically between this point and the collar. Take a stitch with the sewing thread at the collar. To the right of the turtle's neck, on the shell and at the same height as the collar stitch, find a place you would like to attach the other end of the cord. About half way down what is left of the cord, take a stitch with the sewing thread. Loop the other end of the cord back up and under the stitch you just took. Using the crochet hook, pop the knot inside the shell.

14 HEADGEAR FOR JOHN AND PAUL

With black embroidery yarn and steel crochet hook:

R1 6 dc into the ring and pull the ring tight. Mark the last stitch. (6 dc.)

R2 2 dc into each stitch around. (12 dc.)

R3 *1 dc, 2 dc into next stitch, repeat from * 5 more times. (18 dc.)

R4 *2 dc, 2 dc into next stitch, repeat from * 5 more times. (24 dc.)

R5 *3 dc, 2 dc into next stitch, repeat from * 5 more times. (30 dc.)

R6 *4 dc, 2 dc into next stitch, repeat from * 5 more times. (36 dc.)

R7 dc into each stitch around. (36 dc.)
Start working back and forth instead of in rounds: ch 3 and turn

R8 tr into same stitch, ch 2, sl st into next 3 stitches, dc into next 15 stitches, sl st into next 3 stitches, ch 3, 2 tr, turn. (Sideburns created.)

{CONTINUED}

R9 sl st across and down the sides of the tr and previously slipped stitches. Once you are back to the dc, dc into each stitch across. (15 dc.)

Continue until hair is the desired length. Finish off.

15 HEADGEAR FOR GEORGE

With red yarn and the larger crochet hook:

R1 6 dc into the ring and pull the ring tight. Mark the last stitch. (6 dc.)

R2 2 dc into each stitch around. (12 dc.)

R3 *1 dc, 2 dc into next stitch, repeat from * 5 more times. (18 dc.)

R4 *2 dc, 2 dc into next stitch, repeat from * 5 more times. (24 dc)

R5–6 dc into each stitch around. (24 dc.)

R7 In front loops only, *3 dc, 2 dc into next stitch, repeat from * 5 more times. (30 dc.)

R6 Back in both loops, *4 dc, 2 dc into next stitch, repeat from * 5 more times. (36 dc.)

R7 *5 dc, 2 dc into next stitch, repeat from * 5 more times. (42 dc.)

R8 *6 dc, 2 dc into next stitch, repeat from * 5 more times. (48 dc.)

Finish off. With 2 strands of white yarn, sew a line of stem stitch around the outside brim. Fold up edges into a tri-cornered hat shape and tack them in place using the sewing needle and thread. Put the hat on George's head and mark where you want the sideburns to be.

With black embroidery thread and the steel hook, start working the back loops left empty at the inside of the brim. Attach thread to the first stitch with a sl st and evenly distribute 27 dc between marks.

ch 3 and turn.

R1 tr into the same stith, ch 2, sl st into next 3 stitches, dc into next 15 stitches, sl st into next 3 stitches, ch 3, 2 tr, turn. (Sideburns created.)

R2 sl st across and down the sides of the tr and previously slipped stitches. Once you are back to the dc, dc into each stitch across. (15 dc.)

Continue until hair is the desired length. Finish off.

Put a knot in the middle of the 8 cm (3 in) length of bright-green yarn. Unravel both ends of the yarn and tack the knot to the hat with the sewing thread. Now he has a jaunty feather in his hat!

16 HEADGEAR FOR RINGO

With pink yarn and the larger crochet hook:

R1 6 dc into the ring and pull the ring tight. Mark the last stitch. (6 dc.)
R2 2 dc into each stitch around. (12 dc.)
R3 *1 dc, 2 dc into next stitch, repeat from * 5 more times. (18 dc.)
R4 *2 dc, 2 dc into next stitch, repeat from * 5 more times. (24 dc.)
R5 *3 dc, 2 dc into next stitch, repeat from * 5 more times. (30 dc.)
R6 dc into all stitches around. (30 dc.)
R7 *3 dc, dc dec, repeat from * 5 more times. (24 dc.)
R8 In front loops only, dc into all stitches around. (24 dc.)
R9 Back in both loops, dc into all stitches around. (24 dc.)

Finish off. Put the hat on Ringo's head and mark where you want the sideburns to be. With black embroidery thread and the steel hook, start working the back loops of the last row. Attach thread to the first stitch with a sl st and evenly distribute 27 dc between marks.
ch 3 and turn.

R1 tr into the same stitch, ch 2, sl st into next 3 stitches, dc into next 15 stitches, sl st into next 3 stitches, ch 3, 2 tr, turn. (Sideburns created.)
R2 sl st across and down the sides of the tr and previously slipped stitches. Once you are back to the dc, dc into each stitch across. (15 dc.)

Continue until hair is the desired length. Finish off.

17 Put the headgear on the Fab Four and get ready to rock out!

little red riding hood

{www.elisalataster.com} ELISA LATASTER

You hear the words *Once upon a time . . .* and curl up under your blanket. Little Red Riding Hood (Roodkapje) is a fairytale character every child loves. In her little basket is a note that says: 'May love and trust always guide you in the dark woods'.

FINISHED SIZE

- 27 cm × 13 cm (10½ in × 5 in)

TOOLS

- Tracing paper
- Fabric marker
- Scissors
- Pins
- Sewing needle
- Sewing machine
- Stuffing stick (or chopstick)

MATERIALS

- Body fabric – a 50 cm × 30 cm (20 in × 12 in) piece of red polar fleece.
- Extra fabric – scraps of pink felt for the face and hands, and brown felt for the hair and basket; an 18 cm × 12 cm (7 in × 5 in) piece of red and white chequered cotton fabric for the dress.
- Decorations – a 35 cm (14 in) length of 12 mm (½ in) wide red lace ribbon; a 30 cm (12 in) length of 4 cm (1½ in) wide white lace ribbon; a 12 cm (5 in) length of 2 cm (¾ in) wide white lace ribbon; a 12 cm (5 in) length of a patterned ribbon; 3 small fabric flowers for the basket; and 1 large fabric flower for the brooch.
- Thread – coloured sewing thread to match fabric; black embroidery thread for the face details.
- Stuffing – wool rovings or polyfill.

{CONTINUED}

{little red riding hood}

INSTRUCTIONS

1 Trace and cut out the enlarged pattern using the template provided. Pin it to the fabric and cut out the pieces. You will need to cut 2 body shapes, 1 bottom shape, 1 dress shape, 1 face shape, 1 hair shape, 4 hand shapes and 2 basket shapes from your fabric.

2 Pin the 2 body pieces together (right sides facing) and sew from A to B around the body, leaving the base open. Pin the bottom piece to the base (right side facing in) and sew around, leaving an opening for turning right side out and filling (as marked on the pattern). Nick the seam allowance every 3 cm (1 in) all the way around, for a neater finish after turning right side out. Turn body right side out. Roll the seams between your thumb and pointer finger until they lie flat.

3 Using a stuffing stick or your fingers, push small amounts of stuffing into the head first, then use larger amounts to gradually fill the rest of the body until the stuffing is firm and even. (Massage the doll as you are stuffing it, to get an even shape with no lumps.) Sew the stuffing opening closed using a whip stitch.

4 To make the sleeves, cut two 9 cm (3½ in) lengths of the 4 cm (½ in) wide white lace ribbon. Fold each piece of ribbon in half (right sides facing) and stitch the ends together, then sew along the long straight edge. Turn right side out.

5 For each hand, pin 2 pieces together (right sides facing), and sew together using tiny stitches, leaving the straight edge open for turning right side out and stuffing. Use a stuffing stick to fill each hand with little bits of polyfill. Insert each hand into a sleeve and sew along the straight edge, closing the stuffing opening as you go.

6 Use the sewing machine to sew the straight edge of the 2 cm (¾ in) wide white lace ribbon to the straight edge of the remaining 4 cm (1½ in) wide white lace ribbon. Then sew the patterned ribbon to the straight edge of these, just overlapping to cover the existing seam.

7 Make a small hem along the straight edge of the dress shape. Sew the joined ribbons to the bottom of the dress using a single stitch line along the top of the patterned ribbon, so that the lace hangs over the bottom edge of the chequered fabric by 2 cm (¾ in). Tuck the ends of the ribbons under and sew with the sewing machine.

8 Fold the side edges of the dress under and iron, then clip the curves so it sits flat. Pin the dress, sleeves and hands into position on the body (as marked on the pattern). Pin the red lace ribbon around the edge of the dress. Sew around the dress from C to D, securing the ribbon and hands as you go. Attach the large fabric flower at x.

9 Use black embroidery thread to embroider the eyes and mouth onto the face (as marked on the pattern). Pin the face to the body (as marked) and sew on using matching thread. Then sew on the hair piece using matching thread.

10 Sew the 2 basket shapes together using a blanket stitch, but leave the top of the basket open (as marked on the pattern), so you can put a little treasure or note in it. Blanket stitch along each edge of the opening. Sew the small fabric flowers to the front of the basket. Place the bag over one of the doll's hands.

{CONTINUED}

Enlarge template to 200% Seam allowance is included

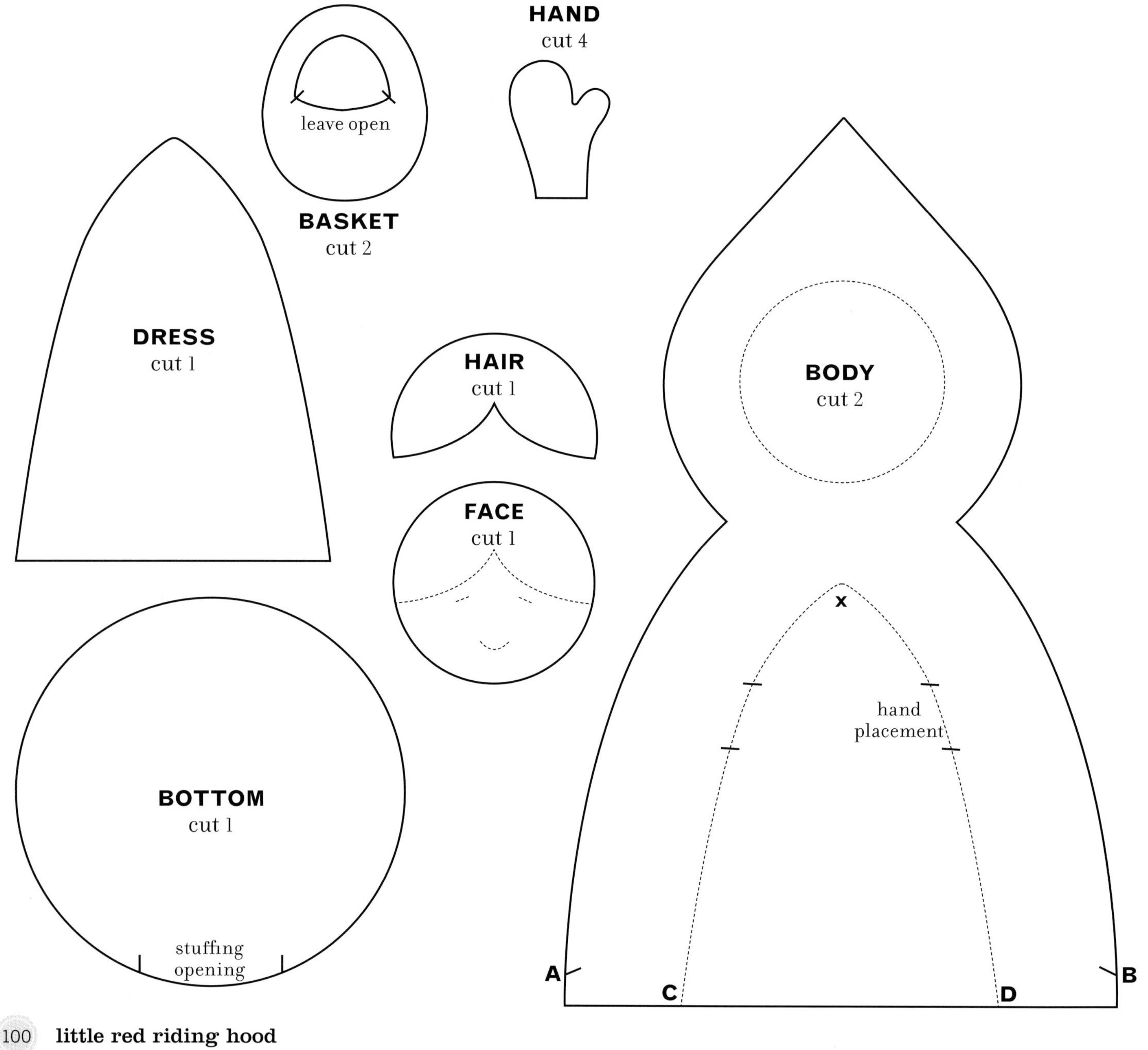

olga elephant

{www.karkovski.typepad.com} KRISTINA KARKOV

This elephant is made using a simple pattern and is suitable for beginners. With some designer or vintage fabric, it really comes to life.

FINISHED SIZE

- 11 cm × 14 cm (4 in × 5½ in)

TOOLS

- Tracing paper
- Fabric marker
- Scissors
- Pins
- Sewing needle
- Sewing machine
- Stuffing stick (or chopstick)

MATERIALS

- Body fabric – a 13 cm × 31 cm (5 in × 12 in) piece of patterned fabric for the body, and a 11 cm × 25 cm (4½ in × 10 in) piece of the same fabric for the gusset and ears.
- Thread – coloured sewing thread to match fabric; embroidery thread or yarn for the eyes.
- Stuffing – polyfill.

{CONTINUED}

INSTRUCTIONS

1 Trace and cut out the pattern using the template provided. Pin it to the fabric and cut out the pieces. You will need to cut 2 body shapes, 1 gusset shape, and 4 ear shapes from your fabric.

2 Pin the 2 body shapes together (right sides facing), and sew from A to B, around the back, head and trunk of the elephant.

3 Pin the gusset piece to the body piece, A to A and B to B, (right sides facing). Sew together, leaving an opening for turning right side out and stuffing (as marked on pattern). Clip all curves close to the stitch line to allow for a smoother finish after turning right side out. Turn right side out.

4 Using a stuffing stick, carefully push small amounts of stuffing into the tight corners first – tail, trunk and legs. Gradually fill the rest of the body until the stuffing is firm and even.

5 Hand sew the stuffing opening closed using a whip stitch.

6 For each ear, pin 2 pieces together (right sides facing), then sew, leaving the straight edge open for turning right side out. Turn right side out. Turn the raw edge under 6 mm (¼ in) and hand sew the opening closed using a ladder stitch. Position ears on the head (as marked on the pattern), and attach with a ladder stitch.

7 Use embroidery thread to sew the eyes: insert the needle at x and push it all the way through the head, coming out on the opposite side, then make a stitch and push it back through the head. Go back and forth through the head a few times so there are several stitches for each eye, pulling the thread tight each time to make the eyes indented. Tie off and hide the thread in the body.

{CONTINUED}

Template shown at 100% Seam allowance is included

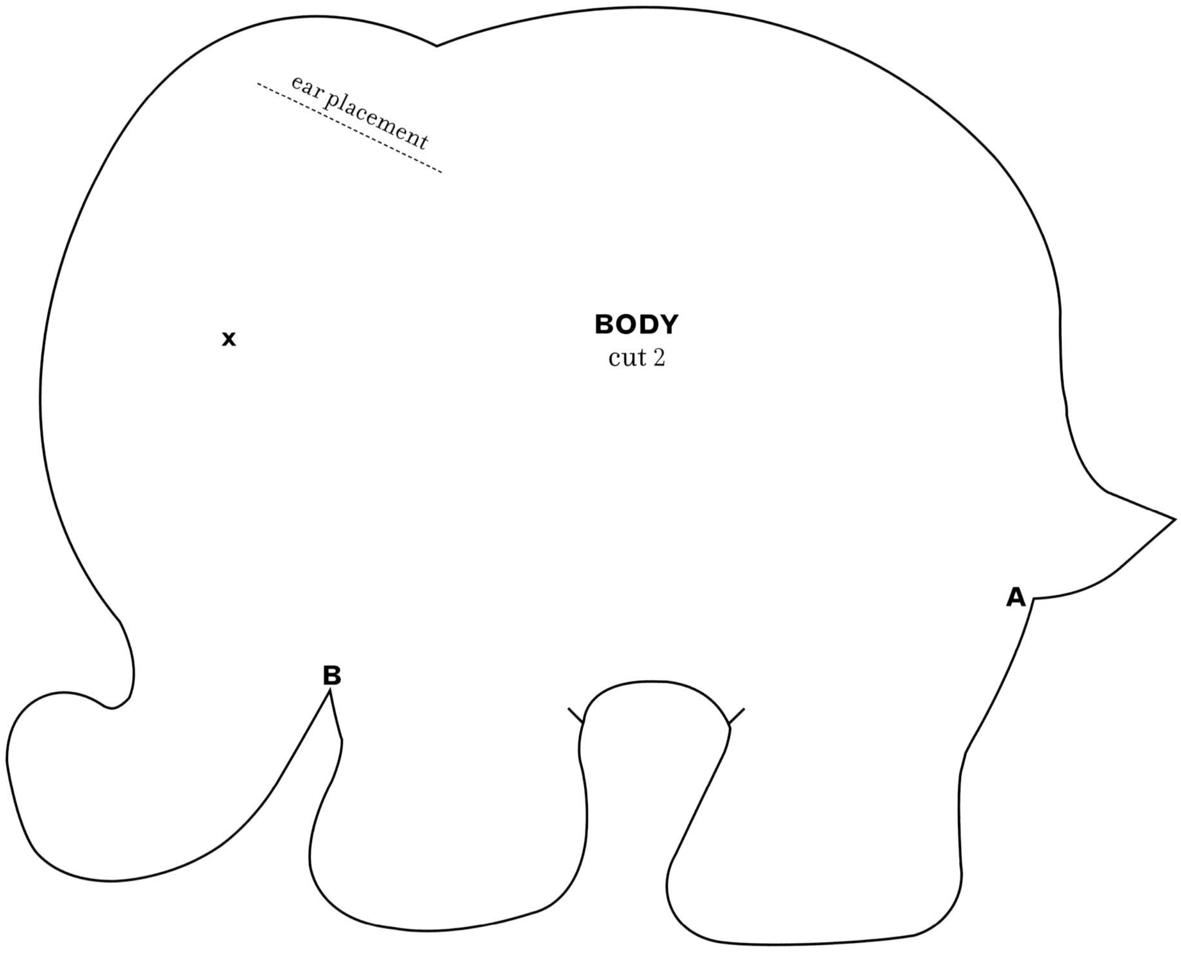

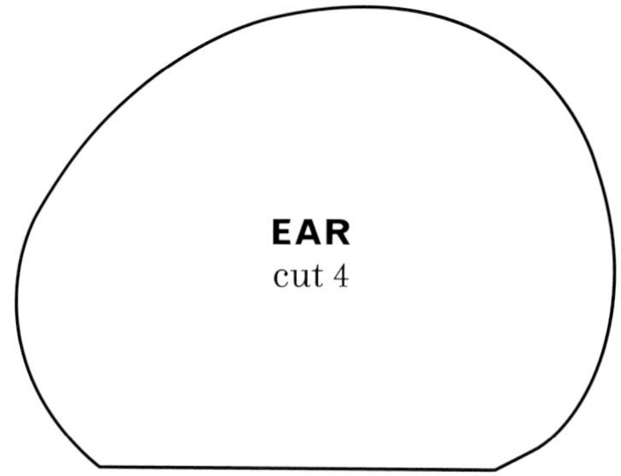
EAR
cut 4

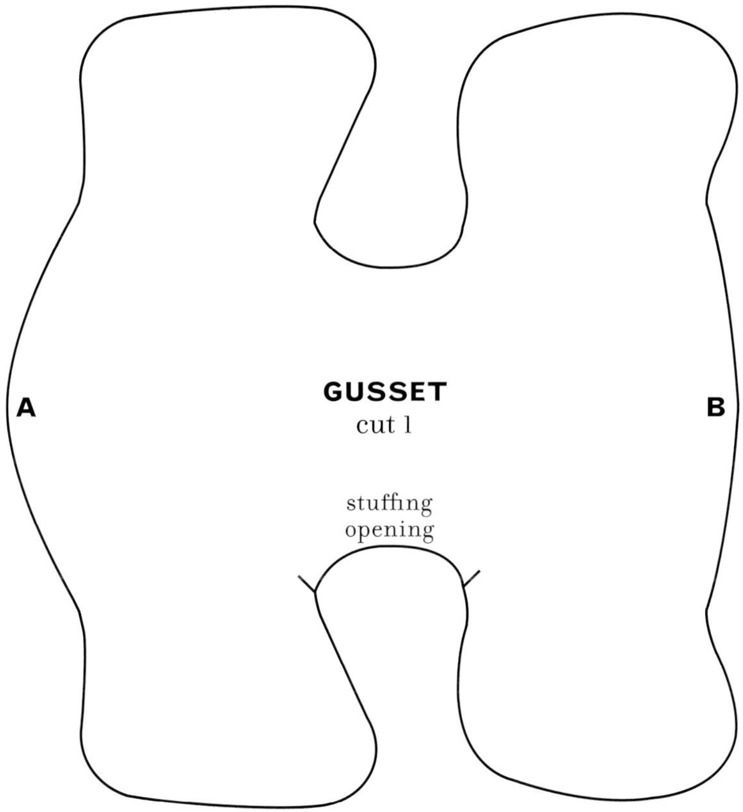
GUSSET
cut 1
A
B
stuffing
opening

owl friend

{H. Luv Fabrications – mciverson.com} HEIDI IVERSON

In the last couple of years I've been obsessed with owls. I paint and draw them all the time. I decided my life wouldn't be complete until I had designed an owl softie. I now have a whole pile of them on my couch – they like to watch cartoons with me. (You can easily make this owl in whatever size you like; just enlarge or shrink the pattern to the desired size.)

FINISHED SIZE

- 22 cm × 13 cm (8½ in × 5 in)

TOOLS

- Tracing paper
- Fabric marker
- Scissors
- Pins
- Embroidery needle
- Sewing machine
- Stuffing stick (or chopstick)

MATERIALS

- Body fabric – a 51 cm × 31 cm (20 in × 12 in) piece of heavy French linen.
- Extra fabric – a 13 cm × 10 cm (5 in × 4 in) piece of lightweight linen for the belly; scraps of felt in 4 or 5 different colours for the eyes, beak and feet.
- Decorations – two coloured buttons for the eyes.
- Thread – coloured sewing thread to match all the fabric colours; pearl cotton or embroidery thread in 10 different colours for the body and eye details.
- Stuffing – polyfill.

{CONTINUED}

{owl friend}

INSTRUCTIONS

1 Trace and cut out the enlarged pattern using the template provided. Pin it to the appropriate fabric and cut out the pieces. You will need to cut 2 body shapes, 1 belly shape, 1 beak shape and 2 foot shapes. For the eyes, cut out 3 or 4 rounds in different sizes and colours (ranging from about 2 cm to 6 cm in diameter) – cut out 2 of each type.

2 Pin the belly shape onto one of the body pieces (as marked on the pattern). Using the sewing machine, zigzag stitch around the belly piece, covering the raw edge of the fabric.

3 For each eye, pin the smallest round on top of the next largest round and sew together on the sewing machine using a straight stitch and matching thread. Pin that piece on top of the next largest round and sew on. Repeat with largest round.

4 Pin the finished eyes to the front of the body (as marked on the pattern). Sew on using straight stitch and matching sewing thread.

5 Pin the beak onto the body (as marked on the pattern) and sew on.

6 Embroider around the edge of the eyes with pearl cotton or embroidery thread in a contrasting colour, using blanket or whip stitch. Using another colour of thread, straight stitch around the second eye layer. Change colours again and embroider an asterisk shape on the top eye layer. Sew a button into the centre of each eye.

7 Embroider the belly of the owl using pearl cotton or embroidery thread in different colours: use a straight stitch to sew an arch shape which follows the belly shape (as shown in the main photograph). Make 5 arches, each time using a different coloured thread and making each arch slightly smaller than the last.

8 Place this front body piece right side up on your work surface. Pin the feet into position (x to x), pointing in towards the body. Place the second body piece right side down on top and pin the 2 pieces together. Sew around the body, securing the feet as you go and remembering to leave an opening for turning right side out and stuffing (as marked on the pattern). Turn right side out.

9 Using a stuffing stick, push small amounts of stuffing into the body until it is firm and even.

10 Hand sew the stuffing opening closed using a whip stitch.

{CONTINUED}

Enlarge template to 200% Seam allowance is included

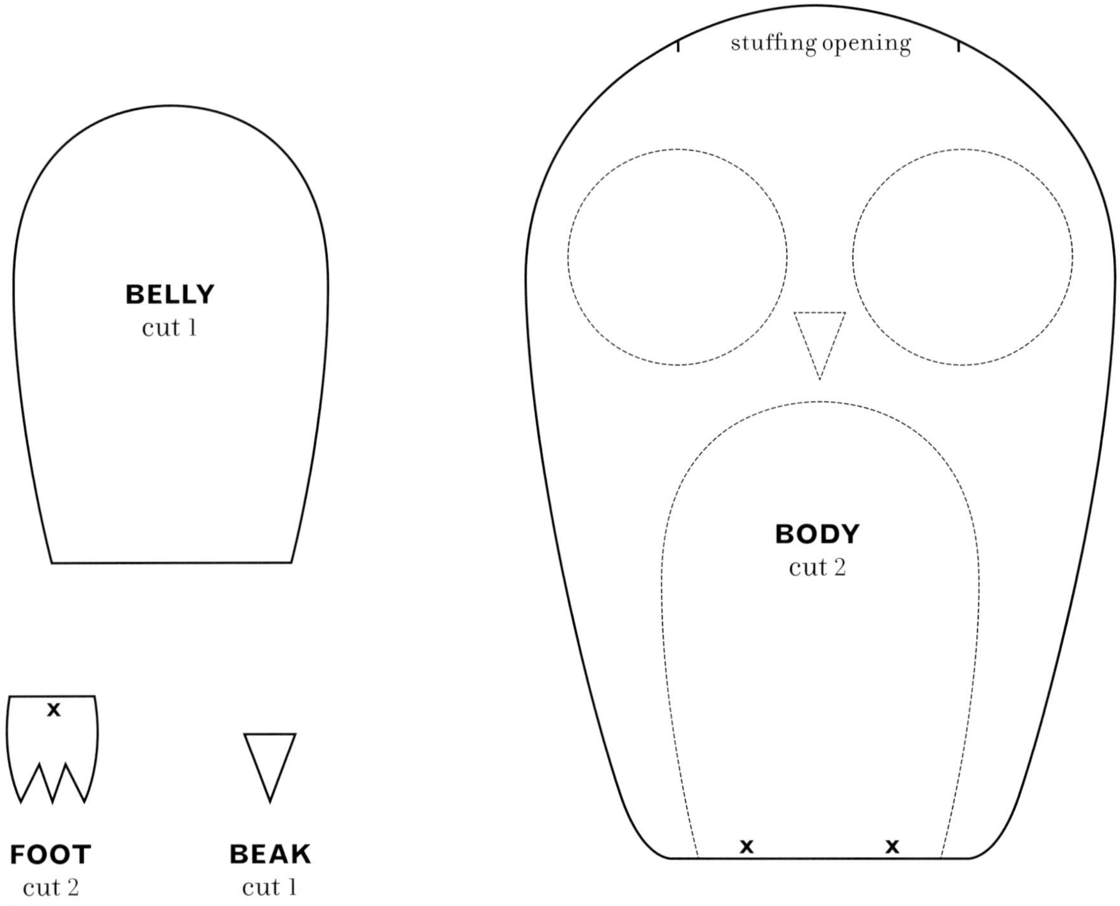

moopy bunny

{Nest Studio – neststudio.typepad.com} CARLY SCHWERDT

Moopy bunnies have moopy cheeks, the kind that make you want to squeeze and kiss and cuddle them. My daughter has moopy cheeks too, as well as a mischievous smile, and she's as cuddly as a bunny . . . hence Moopy Bunny was born. This is the perfect toy to give to your own moopy-cheeked child.

TOOLS

- Tracing paper
- Fabric marker
- Scissors
- Sewing needle
- Sewing machine
- Stuffing stick (or chopstick)
- Iron

MATERIALS

- Body fabric – patterned cotton fabrics in the following sizes: a 15 cm × 15 cm (6 in × 6 in) piece for the head and ears; a 10 cm × 12 cm (4 in × 5 in) piece for the body; a 15 cm × 5 cm (6 in × 2 in) piece for the arms; a 10 cm × 12 cm (4 in × 5 in) piece for the trousers; and a 16 cm × 8 cm (6½ in × 3½ in) piece for the legs. (I like to use brown for Moopy's head and stripes for the legs. Anything you fancy will work for the trousers, body and arms.)
- Extra fabric – a 15 cm × 15 cm (6 in × 6 in) piece of beige felt for the face and ear inserts; a scrap of coloured felt for the bird; a scrap of animal-print fabric and a scrap of plain fabric for the animal toy.
- Thread – brown and rose-coloured cotton thread for embroidering the facial features; sewing thread to match body fabric.
- Stuffing – polyfill.

{CONTINUED}

INSTRUCTIONS

1 Trace and cut out the enlarged pattern using the template provided. Pin it to the appropriate fabric and cut out the pieces. You will need to cut 2 head shapes, 1 face shape, 2 body shapes, 2 trousers shapes, 4 arm shapes, 4 leg shapes and 6 ear shapes (4 in patterned fabric and 2 in felt) from your fabric.

2 Pin the felt face piece to one of the head pieces and sew on. Embroider the eyes, nose and mouth (as marked on the pattern). (You can also embroider cheeks if you want, or make some out of pink felt and sew them on.)

3 For each of the arms and legs, pin the pieces together (right sides facing), then sew, leaving an opening for turning right side out and stuffing (as marked on the pattern). Turn each limb right side out.

4 For each ear, pin together 2 patterned ear pieces (right sides facing) and a felt ear piece. (The felt inserts give the ears just enough stiffness to make them stand up, without adding too much bulk.) Sew together, leaving the straight edge open for turning right side out. Turn ears right side out, so the felt is on the inside.

5 Pin each body shape to a trousers shape, A to A and B to B, (right sides facing), then sew. Then pin and sew each body shape to a head shape, C to C and D to D, (right sides facing).

6 Place the front body piece right side up on your work surface. Pin the ears, arms and legs into position (x to x, y to y and z to z), pointing in towards the body and remembering which way they will face when the body is turned right side out. Make sure the stuffing openings in the limbs end up on the underside of the arms and the insides of the legs (so they show the least). Place the second body piece right side down on top and pin the two body pieces together. Sew, securing the limbs and ears in place as you go, and leaving an opening for turning right side out and stuffing (as marked). (If you're making the toy for a child, you may like to double or triple stitch where the arms, legs and ears are attached, to make them stronger.) Trim around the edges with scissors, and nick fabric around the curves, to allow for a smoother finish after turning right side out. Be careful not to clip the seam. Turn right side out.

{CONTINUED}

7 Using a stuffing stick, push small amounts of stuffing into the head and work your way down (it's important to use very small amounts, and pack them tightly, to avoid creating lumps). Fill the body until the stuffing is firm and even, then stuff the arms and legs. Sew all the stuffing openings closed using a whip stitch.

8 To make the little bird, use the pattern to cut 2 bird shapes out of felt, then sew together by hand, leaving a 15 mm opening in the base for turning right side out and stuffing. Turn right side out, stuff (not too firmly), then sew the stuffing opening closed.

9 To make a toy for Moopy (like the elephant in the photograph), find a fabric with a large animal print and cut around an animal, leaving a 10 mm seam allowance. Pin this to a plain piece of fabric (right sides facing) and cut around the edge, then sew the two pieces together by hand, leaving a 15 mm opening for turning right side out and stuffing. Turn right side out, stuff (not too firmly), then sew the stuffing opening closed.

Enlarge template to 200% Seam allowance is included

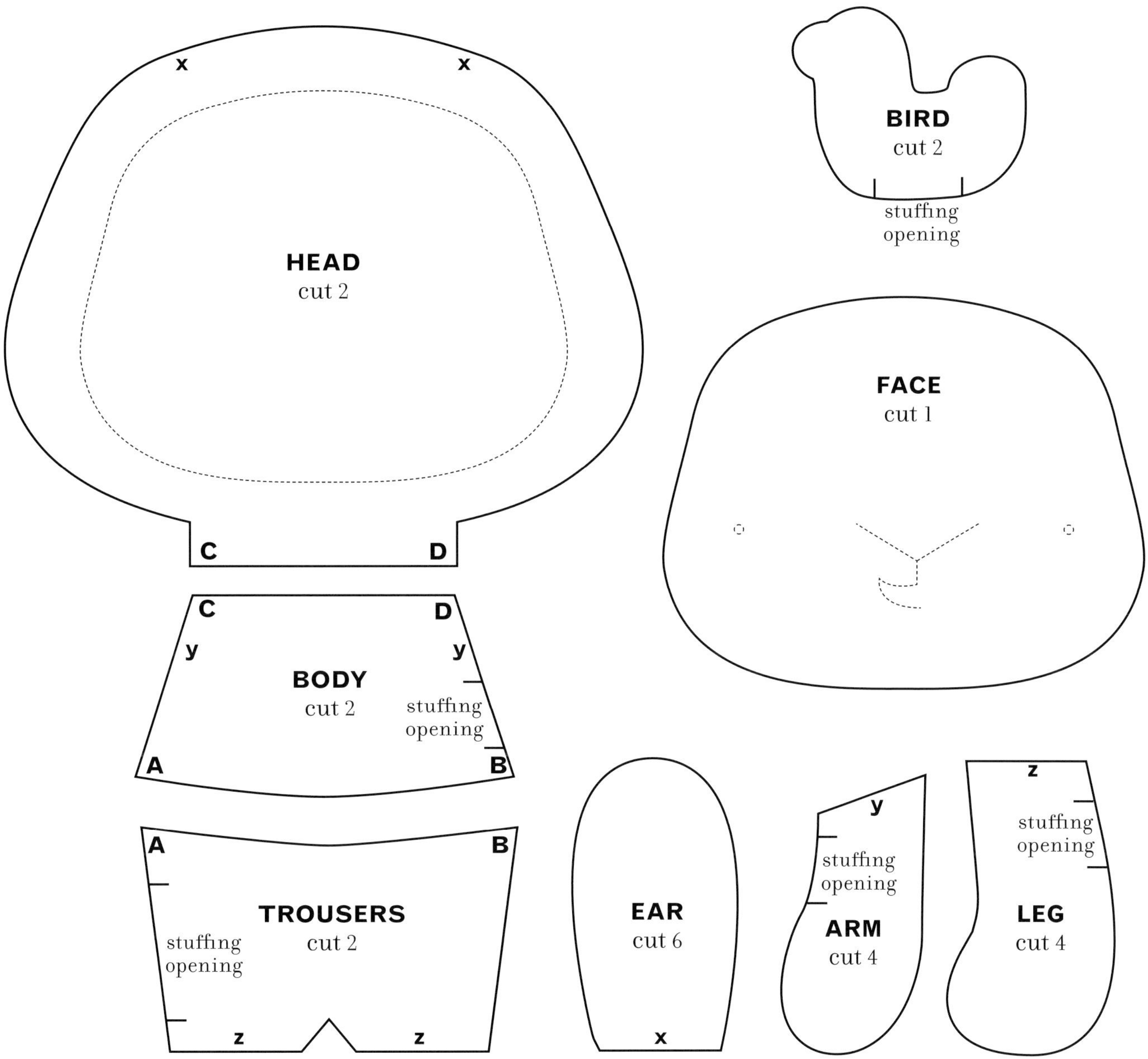

piggy bed warmer

{Soozs – www.soozs.blogspot.com} SUZIE FRY

Like lots of kids, my daughter likes to take a warm wheat pack to bed with her (even when it isn't very cold). I think half the comfort comes from the funny squishy-bumpy texture of the wheat inside the fabric. I decided that if she was going to get attached to a bag of wheat it might as well look cute, so I made this piggy. It's now her constant companion in and out of bed. Just pop piggy in the microwave for a couple of minutes for instant warmth.

FINISHED SIZE

- 33 cm × 27 cm (13 in × 10½ in)

TOOLS

- Tracing paper
- Fabric marking pen
- Scissors
- Pins
- Sewing machine
- Turning stick (or chopstick)
- Sewing needle
- Funnel

MATERIALS

- Body fabric – a 50 cm × 60 cm (20 in × 24 in) piece of fabric for the body. I think a textured fabric is best for feel and heat distribution, so corduroy or towelling work well. (I have used vintage white cotton chenille.)
- Extra fabric – a 10 cm × 15 cm (4 in × 6 in) piece of contrast fabric for the snout and ear inserts. (I have used pink cotton chenille, but wool felt or any cotton or wool fabric would work fine.) A 15 cm × 15 cm (6 in × 6 in) piece of black pure wool felt for the trotters.
- Stuffing – approximately 1 kg of whole wheat grain (you can use culinary or pet feed).
- Thread – coloured sewing thread to match the body fabric, snout and ears, and black to match the trotters; black embroidery thread for the nostrils, eyes and tail.

{CONTINUED}

{piggy bed warmer}

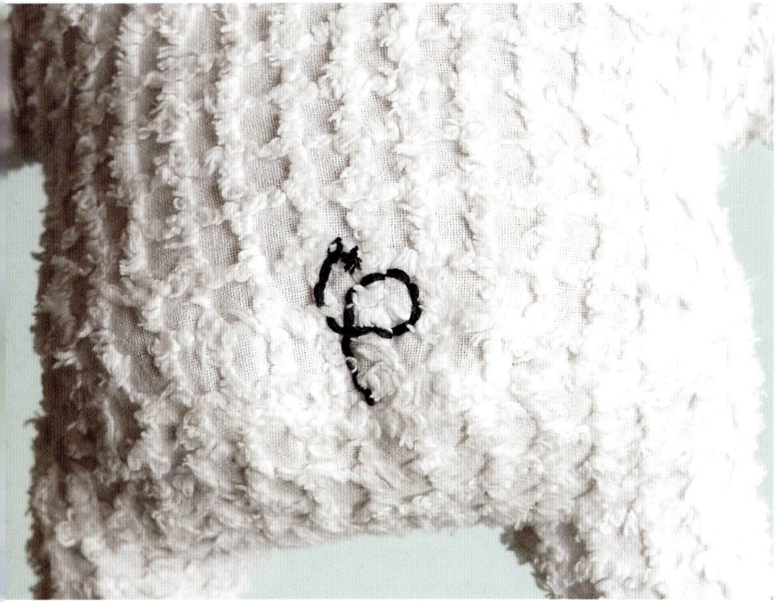

INSTRUCTIONS

1 Trace and cut out the enlarged pattern using the template provided. Pin it to the appropriate fabric and cut out the pieces. (Pay attention to the grain of the fabric and make sure the fabric is oriented in the same direction for all pattern pieces.) You will need to cut 1 of each body shape (front, back and lower body), 2 inner ear shapes, 1 snout shape, 4 hand trotter shapes and 4 foot trotter shapes from your fabric.

2 Using embroidery thread, embroider a few straight stitches on the snout to make nostrils (as marked on the pattern). Using a very tight zigzag stitch or appliqué stitch on the sewing machine, sew the snout to the front body shape (as marked). Embroider the eyes in black, using satin stitch (as marked). Attach inner ear pieces using a very tight zigzag or appliqué stitch (as marked).

3 Pin the back body piece and the lower body piece together, A to A and B to B, (right sides facing). Sew from A to B, leaving an opening for turning right side out and stuffing (as marked on the pattern). Pin the front body piece to this back body piece so the arms, legs and ears match up (right sides facing), then sew together. Trim the points of the ears and nick around the curved edges for a smoother finish after turning right side out. Turn right side out, using a turning stick for the tight corners if necessary.

4 Using the funnel, fill the body with wheat. Sew the stuffing opening closed using a whip stitch.

5 For each of the trotters, pin the 2 matching pieces together (right sides facing), and sew, leaving the straight edge open for turning right side out. Turn right side out. Place each trotter over one of the pig's hands or feet and sew in place using back stitch.

6 Using a simple back stitch and black embroidery thread, embroider a curly tail on the pig's bottom (as marked on the pattern).

{CONTINUED}

Enlarge template to 200% Seam allowance is included

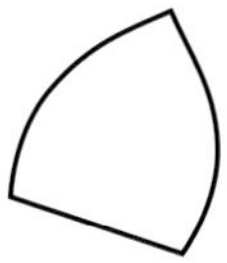

INNER EAR
cut 2

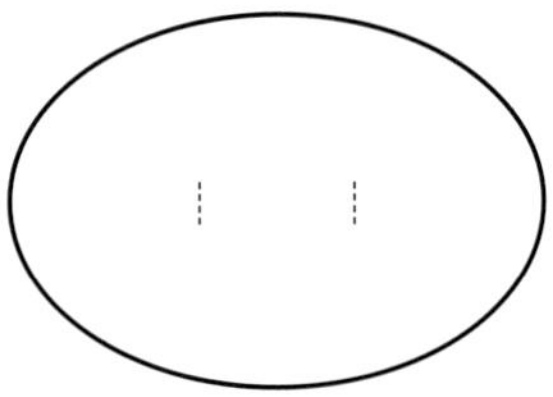

SNOUT
cut 1

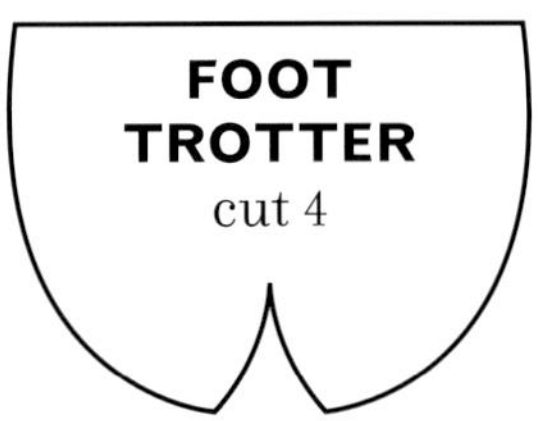

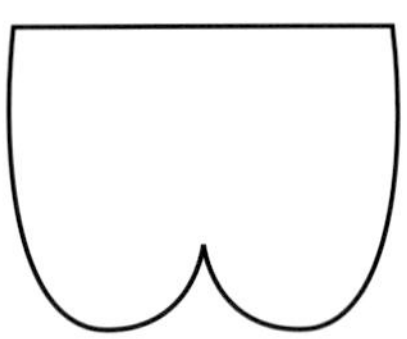

HAND TROTTER
cut 4

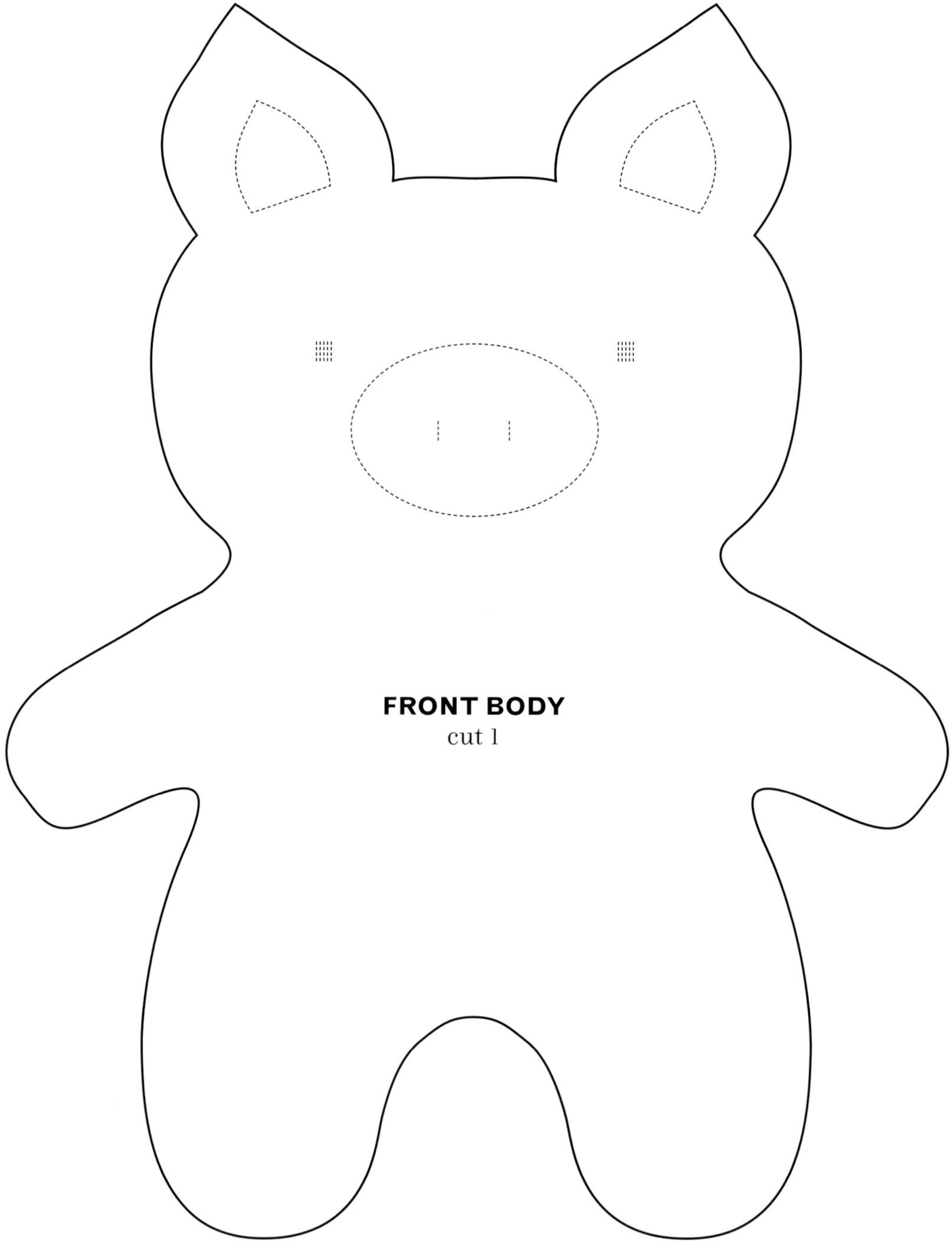

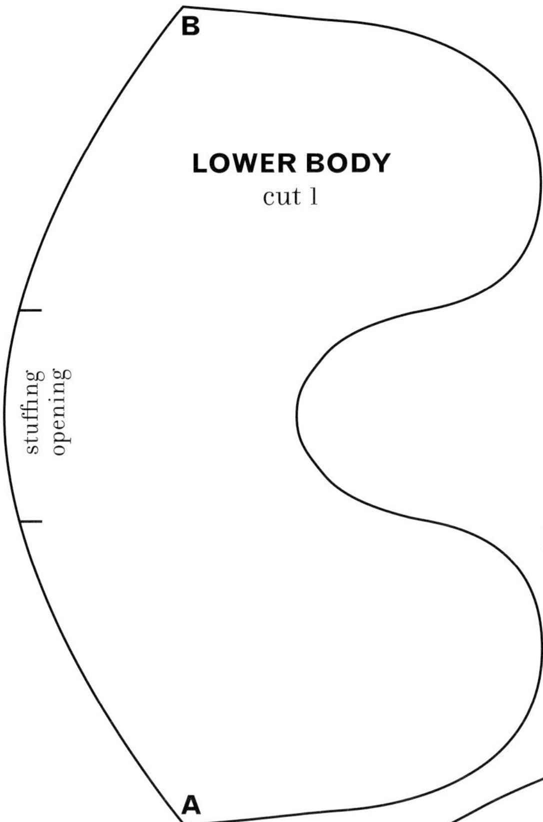
B
LOWER BODY
cut 1
stuffing opening
A

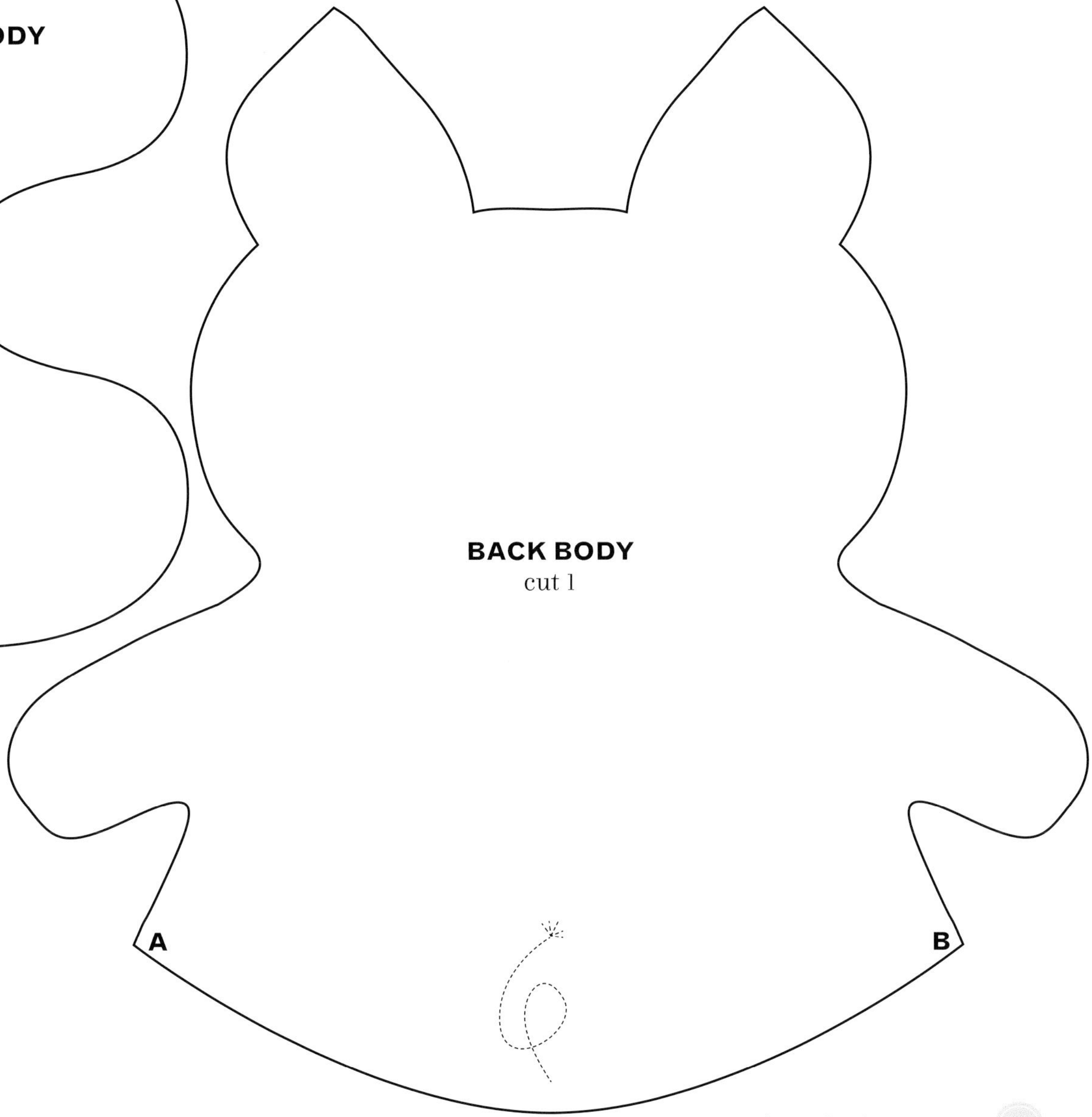
BACK BODY
cut 1
A
B

maisie

{neverenoughhours.blogspot.com} KATE HENDERSON

Maisie will make a wonderful little friend for any child. If the doll is for a child under three years of age, make it without the felt cheeks and flowers.

FINISHED SIZE

- 28 cm (11 in) × 18 cm (7 in)

TOOLS

- Tracing paper
- Fabric marker
- Scissors
- Pins
- Sewing needle
- Sewing machine
- Stuffing stick (or chopstick)
- Iron
- Flower punch (optional)

MATERIALS

- Body fabric – a 40 cm × 15 cm (16 in × 6 in) piece of patterned fabric for the head; a 38 cm × 15 cm (15 in × 6 in) piece of patterned fabric for the upper body; a 38 cm × 7 cm (15 in × 3 in) piece of patterned fabric for the lower body.
- Extra fabric – a 15 cm × 25 cm (6 in × 10 in) piece of patterned fabric for the legs and arms; small pieces of felt in 2 colours for the face, flowers and cheeks.
- Decorations – a 35 cm (13 in) length of ric rac or ribbon.
- Thread – coloured sewing thread to match the body fabric; embroidery thread in black, plus colours to match the felt.
- Stuffing – polyfill.

{CONTINUED}

{maisie}

INSTRUCTIONS

1 Trace and cut out the enlarged pattern using the template provided. Pin it to the appropriate fabric and cut out the pieces. You will need to cut 2 head shapes, 2 upper body shapes, 2 lower body shapes, 4 arm shapes, 4 leg shapes, 1 face shape, and 2 cheek shapes from your fabric.

2 Use satin stitch to embroider the eyes onto the face with 2 strands of black embroidery thread and use split stitch to embroider the eyelashes, nose and mouth (as marked on the pattern). Sew on the cheek pieces using a single cross-stitch in the centre of each round. Use a straight stitch and matching embroidery thread to sew the face to the head.

3 Pin each upper body piece to a lower body piece, A to A and B to B (right sides facing), then sew from A to B. Iron seams flat. Cut the length of ric rac or ribbon in half and sew each piece onto the body to cover the seam where the body pieces join. Pin a head piece to each body piece, C to C and D to D, (right sides facing), and sew from C to D.

4 For each arm, pin 2 arm shapes together (right sides facing), then sew, leaving the straight end open for turning right side out and stuffing. Repeat for the legs. Turn each limb right side out and iron. Use a stuffing stick to stuff each arm and leg.

5 Place the front body piece right side up on your work surface. Baste the arms and legs in position on the body (x to x and y to y), pointing in towards the body and remembering which way they will face when the body is turned right side out. Place the second body piece right side down on top and pin the 2 body pieces together. Sew, securing the arms and legs in place as you go and leaving an opening for turning right side out and stuffing (as marked). Turn body right side out and iron.

6 Using a stuffing stick, push small amounts of stuffing into the head first. Gradually fill the rest of the body until the stuffing is firm and even. Hand stitch the stuffing opening closed using a ladder stitch.

7 Use the flower punch to make 2 flowers out of felt, or use the flower template to cut out 2 flower shapes. Use embroidery thread to secure each flower to the head using a single cross-stitch (as marked on the pattern).

{CONTINUED}

Template shown at 100% Seam allowance is included

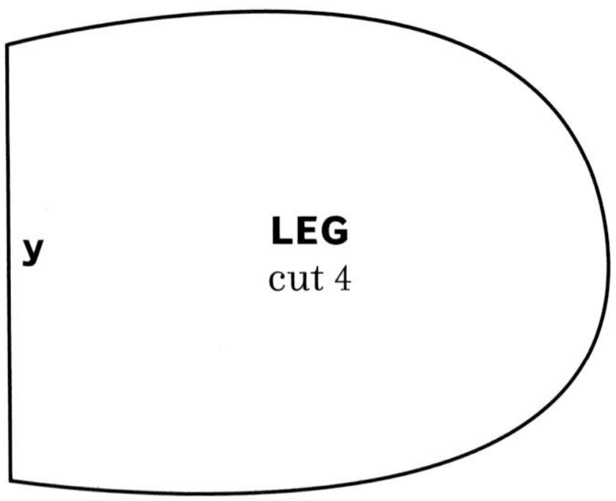

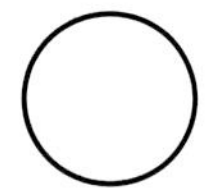

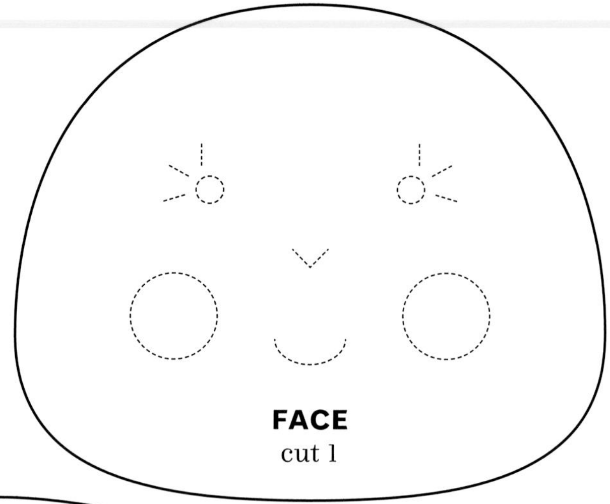

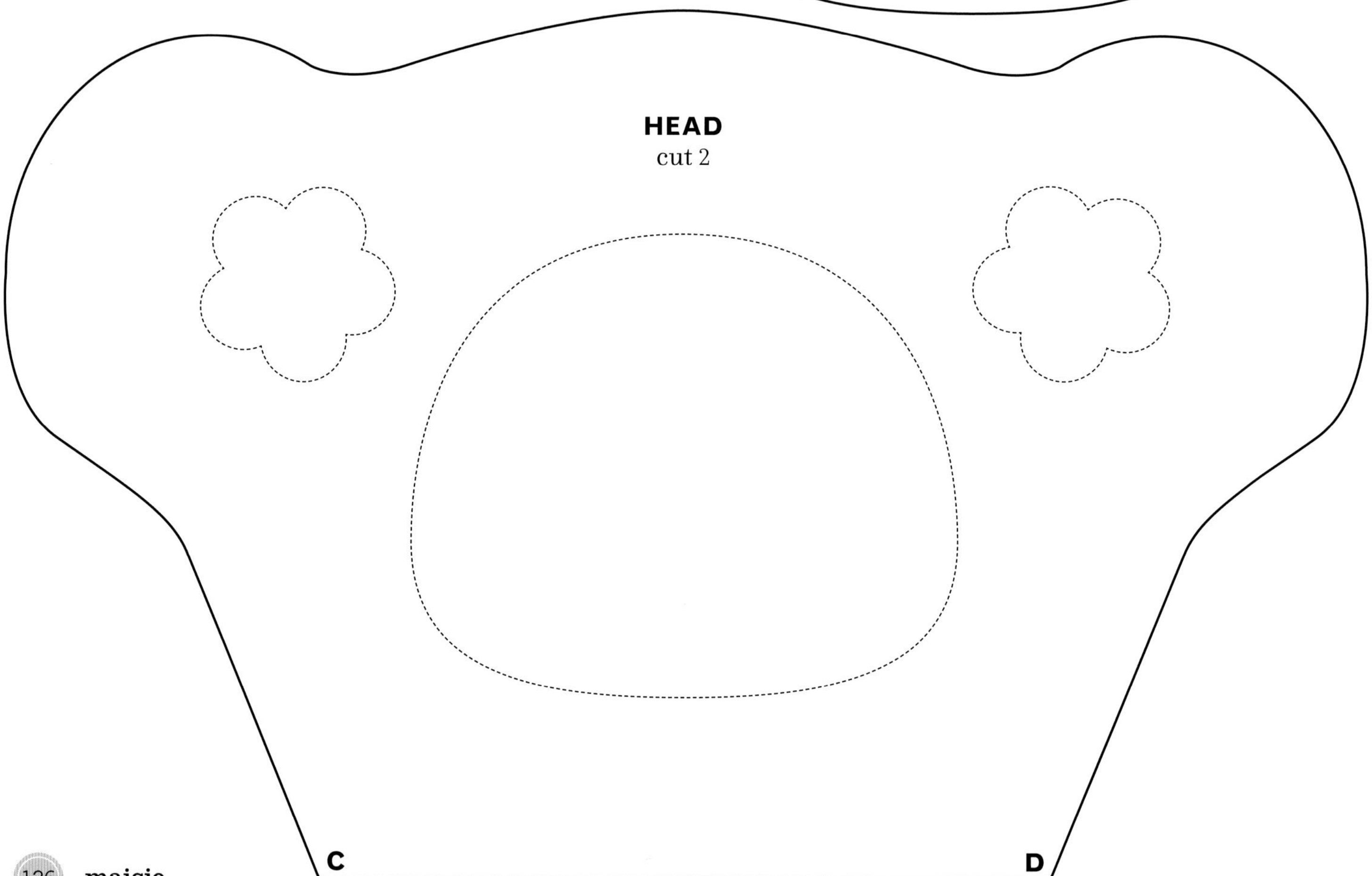

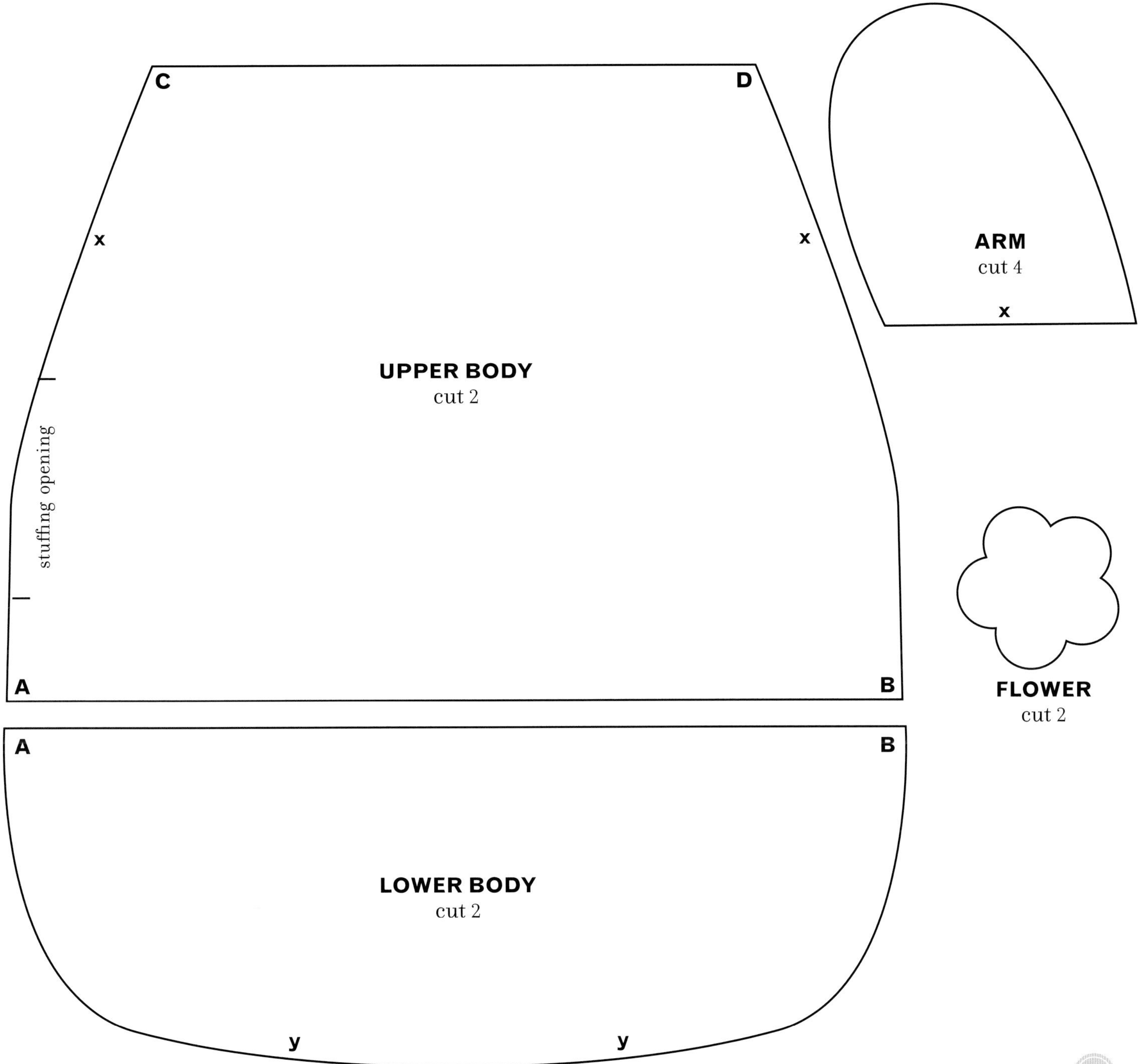
C
D
x
x
ARM
cut 4
x
UPPER BODY
cut 2
stuffing opening
A
B
FLOWER
cut 2
A
B
LOWER BODY
cut 2
y
y

the princess & the pea

{redfeltflower.blogspot.com} SARAH BOWE

This play-set is based on the much-loved fairytale by Hans Christian Anderson. Children will have a ball piling up the mattresses and trying to find the pea.

FINISHED SIZE

- Mattresses: 15 cm (h) × 19 cm (w) × 29 cm (l) (6 in × 7½ in × 11½ in)
- Princess: 17 cm × 6 cm (7 in × 2½ in)
- Pea: 2 cm (¾ in)

TOOLS

- Tracing paper
- Fabric marker
- Scissors
- Pins
- Sewing needle
- Sewing machine
- Iron
- Stuffing stick (or chopstick)

MATERIALS

- Mattress fabric – assorted fabrics (denim, linen, cotton ticking, tea towels, cotton quilt fabrics, vintage fabrics) cut to the following sizes: 4 pieces measuring 22 cm × 30 cm (8½ in × 12 in); 4 pieces measuring 21 cm × 29 cm (8 in × 11½ in); 4 pieces measuring 20 cm × 28 cm (8 in × 11 in); 4 pieces measuring 19 cm × 27 cm (7½ in × 10½ in); 4 pieces measuring 18 cm × 26 cm (7 in × 10 in); 4 pieces measuring 17 cm × 25 cm (6½ in × 10 in). (Experienced sewers may like to piece together smaller pieces of fabric to make up the sizes required for the mattresses, to create a patchwork effect).
- Doll fabric – a 14 cm × 17 cm (5½ in × 6½ in) piece of patterned fabric for the body; 2 pieces calico measuring 10.5 cm × 17 cm (4 in × 6½ in) for the doll's head; a 10.5 cm × 17 cm (4 in × 6½ in) piece of brown wool felt for the doll's hair; a 2 cm × 16 cm (¾ in × 6 in) piece of red wool felt for the doll's collar.
- Extra fabric – two pieces of denim, each measuring 10 cm × 14 cm (4 in × 5½ in), for the pillow; 2 pieces of patterned fabric measuring 20 cm × 28 cm (8 in × 11 in)

{CONTINUED}

for the blanket; a 10 cm × 10 cm (4 in × 4 in) piece of green wool felt for the pea.

- Thread – embroidery thread in 4 colours: chocolate-brown for the doll's hair; black for the doll's eyes; red for the doll's mouth and collar; green for the pea.
- Decorations – a button to adorn the doll's collar.
- Stuffing – polyfill or wool rovings; cotton quilt batting to fill the mattresses.

INSTRUCTIONS

1 For each of the 12 mattresses, pin together 2 matching pieces of fabric (right sides facing). Sew together using the sewing machine, leaving a 10 cm (4 in) opening on the shorter side for turning right side out and inserting the quilt batting. Use scissors to trim each of the 4 corners diagonally across, being carefully not to clip the seam, then turn right side out. Gently push out the corners with a stuffing stick. Iron lightly. Fill each mattress with a piece of batting slightly smaller than the mattress size (alternatively you can use soft filling, or a combination of both). Sew the stuffing openings closed using a slip stitch.

2 Pin the 2 pieces of pillow fabric together (right sides facing) and sew, leaving a 5 cm (2 in) opening for turning right side out and stuffing. Use scissors to trim each of the 4 corners diagonally across, being careful not to clip the seam, then turn right side out. Fill with polyfill or wool rovings. Sew the stuffing opening closed using a slip stitch.

3 Pin the 2 pieces of blanket fabric together (right sides facing) and sew together, leaving a 10 cm (4 in) opening for turning right side out. Trim each of the 4 corners diagonally across, then turn right side out. Sew the opening closed using a slip stitch.

4 Trace and cut out the enlarged pattern using the template provided. Pin it to the appropriate fabric and cut out the pieces. You will need to cut 1 body shape, 2 head shapes, 1 hair shape, 1 collar shape and 1 pea shape from your fabric.

5 Treat the 2 head pieces as if they are one piece of fabric (using a double thickness for the doll's head prevents the embroidery threads from showing through). Pin together the body piece and the head pieces, A to A and B to B, (right sides facing). Sew from A to B. Iron seam flat.

6 Position hair shape on the right side of the head piece (as marked on the pattern). With chocolate-brown embroidery thread, attach the hair to the head using a back stitch (as marked).

7 Embroider the mouth using 6 strands of red embroidery thread, then use 6 strands of black embroidery thread to make French knots for the eyes (as marked on the pattern).

8 With panels running horizontally, fold the stitched body/head piece in half (right sides facing) and machine stitch along the long edge, leaving a 10 mm (⅖ in) seam allowance. Gently iron seam flat. Machine stitch along the bottom edge of the body, leaving a 2 cm (¾ in) seam allowance. Turn right side out. Use a stuffing stick to stuff the doll firmly.

9 Position the collar shape along the top seam where the body joins the head, with the ends meeting in the

{CONTINUED}

centre of the front. Use back stitch and 3 strands of red embroidery thread to stitch along the top edge of the collar to secure (as marked on the pattern). Finish by attaching a pretty button (as shown in the photographs).

10 Turn the brown felt (hair) under 2.5 cm (1 in) inside the doll and use a slip stitch to neatly sew up the top of the head.

11 To make the pea, use 3 strands of green embroidery thread to sew a straight stitch around the edge of the green felt round, sewing 10 mm ($\frac{2}{5}$ in) from the edge and leaving at least a 10 cm (4 in) tail at each end of the thread. Turn the round over so that the long threads are on the underside. Place a small ball of stuffing in the centre of the round and turn the 10 mm edge in to the centre. Gently pull the long threads tight so that the edges gather together to make a ball (make sure the 10-mm edge stays tucked inside). Tie the long threads together in a knot, then stitch them in to finish.

Enlarge template to 200% Seam allowance is included

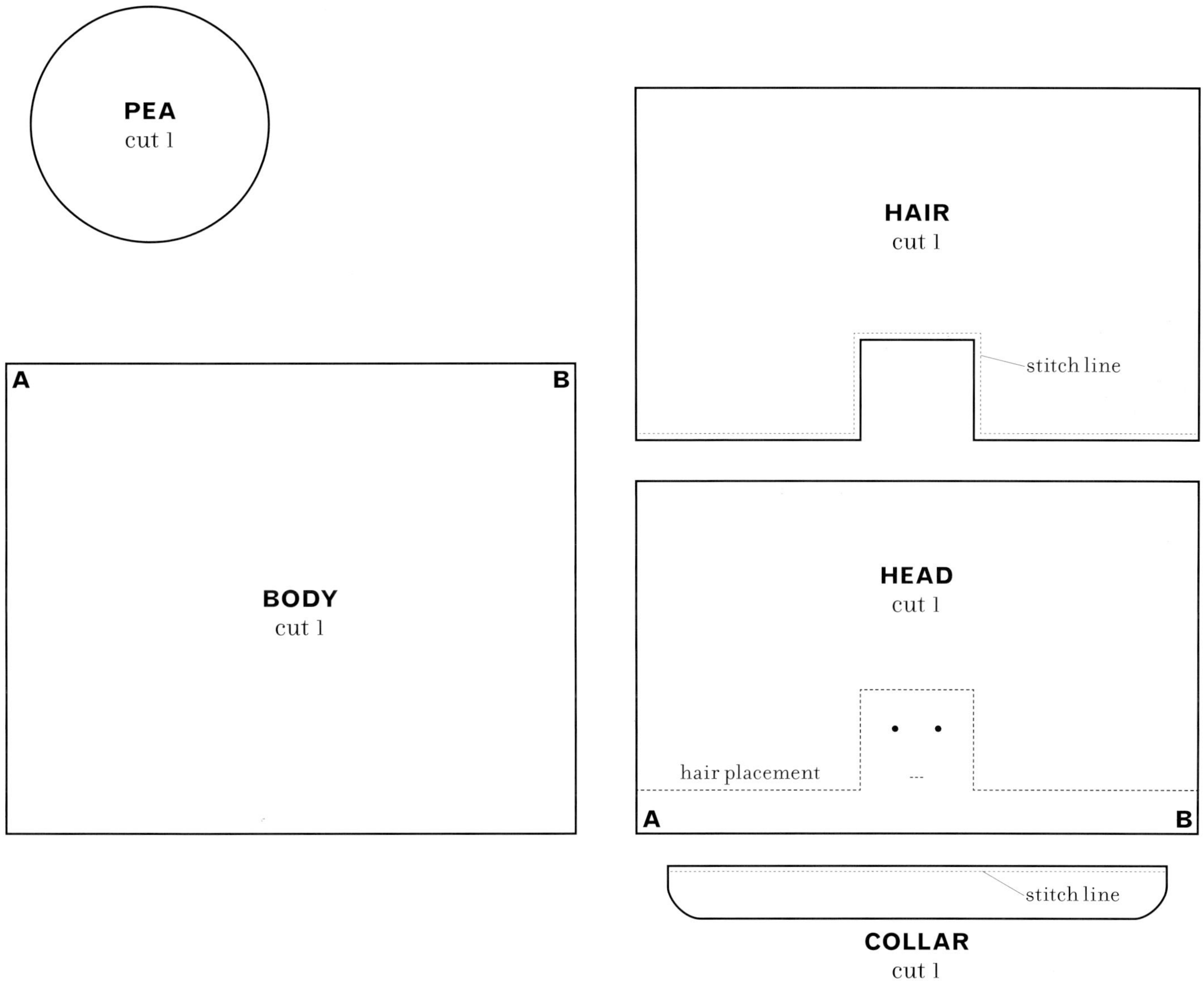

55
56 57

glossary

Back stitch Work from right to left. Pass needle up from underside of fabric, then insert it about 3 mm (1/10 in) to the right of this point. Bring needle up again about 3 mm to the left of the starting point. Continue in this manner.

Basting The action of sewing large removable stitches by hand or machine, in order to hold fabrics in place before sewing securely. To baste two pieces of fabric together by hand, make a series of very large running stitches along the seam line, taking several stitches on your needle before pulling the thread through. Secure with two back stitches close together. Once you've decided that the seam is appropriate, stitch the fabric permanently, then carefully unpick the back stitches and remove the basting thread.

Blanket stitch (For edging fabric.) Work from left to right. Pass needle up through underside of fabric. Insert the needle to the right of this point, parallel to the edge of the fabric. Pull the thread almost all the way through, then insert the needle through the loop from underneath. Insert the needle to the right of the last stitch, and repeat this process. Continue in this manner.

Chain stitch (ch) Yarn over hook, then pull yarn through stitch on hook.

Clipping the seam allowance Curved seams should be clipped so that they will be smooth when turned right side out and stuffed. After sewing, trim edges, but leave at least a 10 mm border. With scissors, nick fabric around the curved edges (tight curves will need more nicks). Be careful to not clip the seam. Outer curves should be 'notched', whereby you clip a small triangle out of the seam allowance.

Cut on the fold Fold your fabric in half before cutting out the piece from the pattern, with the folded line positioned as marked on the pattern. You will end up with a pattern piece of double thickness, joined down one side by the fold.

Double crochet (dc) Insert hook into next stitch, then yarn over hook. Pull yarn through stitch (so there's 2 loops on the hook), then yarn over hook and pull yarn through both loops on hook.

French knot Pass needle up from underside of fabric, at the point where the knot is to lie. Wrap the thread around the needle several times, then insert needle very close to where it came up. Pull tight to secure.

(CONTINUED)

{glossary}

Freezer paper A coated paper that can be ironed onto fabric, and can be removed easily without leaving marks. Used as an alternative to tracing paper when cutting out templates.

Fusible interfacing An adhesive interfacing for stiffening non-stuffed parts such as ears.

Fusible web Double-sided adhesive paper used to stick one piece of fabric to another.

Half treble crochet (htr) Yarn over hook, then insert hook into next stitch. Pull yarn through stitch (so there's 3 loops on the hook), then yarn over hook and pull yarn through all 3 loops on hook.

Knit stitch (knitting) Insert right needle through front of the first stitch on the left needle. Wrap yarn around tip of right needle, then use the right needle to draw the yarn through the stitch on the left needle. Slip original stitch off the left needle. Continue in this manner.

Ladder stitch Line up fabrics to be joined side by side. Pass needle up from underside of first fabric, then insert parallel into second fabric. Bring needle up again about 3 mm ($\frac{1}{10}$ in) along on the second fabric. Insert needle parallel into first fabric. Continue in this manner. (The stitches should be almost invisible.)

Ric rac A type of ribbon.

Right sides facing When sewing, you place pieces of fabric with their 'pretty' sides facing each other (i.e. the sides that will eventually face out). You sew on the 'wrong' side of the fabric so that the seams will be hidden when the piece is turned right side out.

Running stitch Push the needle in and out of the fabric in a straight line, along the edge of the seam. Make stitches on the top of equal length, and stitches on the underside also of equal length, but about half as long as the stitches on the top.

Satin stitch Use consecutive straight stitches, very close together, across the entire shape to be filled.

Slip stitch (sewing) Used to join folded edges of fabric. (Work from right to left.) Pass needle up through folded edge of first piece of fabric, then pick up a few threads from the folded edge of the second piece of fabric. Pick up a few threads on the first piece. Continue in this manner. (The stitches should be almost invisible.)

Slip stitch (sl st) (crochet) Insert hook into next stitch, then yarn over hook and pull yarn through both loops on hook.

Split stitch Work from left to right. Pass needle up from underside of fabric, then make a small back stitch to the right, passing the needle up between the two plies of working thread. Continue in this manner.

Stem stitch Work from left to right. Pass needle up from underside of fabric to the left of the working line, then insert it about 6 mm (¼ in) to the right on the other side of the working line. Bring it up again on the other side of the line, about 3 mm (1⁄10 in) to the right of your starting point. Continue in this manner.

Straight stitch Single spaced stitches.

Treble crochet (tr) Yarn over hook, then insert hook into next stitch. Pull yarn through stitch (so there are 3 loops on hook), then yarn over hook and pull yarn through 2 loops on hook. Yarn over hook and pull yarn through 2 loops on hook again.

Trimming the seam allowance *See* Clipping the seam allowance.

Turning chain Turn the work so your hook is at the beginning of the next row. Crochet one or more chain stitches, as specified in the pattern.

Whip stitch Work from right to left. Pass needle up from underside of first piece of fabric, then insert needle a little to the left on the second piece of fabric to make a diagonal stitch. Bring needle up parallel on the first piece of fabric. Continue in this manner. (Stitches should be as small as possible.)

Thanks – to the incredibly talented crafters from around the globe who have contributed their stunning work to this book.

fabric credits

Every effort has been made to trace and acknowledge fabric designers and manufacturers. The publisher would be pleased to hear from any copyright holders who have not been acknowledged.

Car & Caravan The red and white polka dot fabric is 100 per cent cotton from Spotlight. The toadstool fabric is from Cosmo Textiles Ltd.

Victor Giraffe Body fabric is vintage.

Elsie the Little Dog Wool blend fabric is from Spotlight. Cotton fabric is from the 'Freshcut' collection by Heather Bailey for Free Spirit Fabrics.

Mister Rooster Wool felt is from De Witte Engel (www.witteengel.nl). Denim is from vintage jeans.

Circus Elephant The leg fabric is vintage. Body fabric is white canvas. Ear fabric is 'Seedlings, Marigold' from 'Flea Market Fancy' by Denyse Schmidt.

Smirky The body fabric is a grey piqué interlock. The inner ear fabric is a vintage striped jersey. The nose fabric is 'Pink Ta Dot' by Michael Miller.

Topsy-turvy Tabitha Day dress fabric is a 100 per cent cotton 1930's reproduction feedsack print by Windham Fabrics. The nightgown fabric is vintage flannelette.

Robot Bear Face mask is a vintage neck tie.

Little Pup Print fabric is 'Project by Cotton, Kobayashi', made in Japan.

Patchwork Horse Leg, mane and tail fabric is white linen. For the patchwork: the green, dark-brown floral, and white and brown stripes are all vintage; the yellow is 'Seedlings, Marigold' from 'Flea Market Fancy' by Denyse Schmidt; and the orange is 'Flowers on Orange' from 'Lightning Bugs and Other Mysteries' by Heather Ross for Free Spirit Fabrics.

Little Red Riding Hood All fabrics are vintage or thrifted (second-hand).

Olga Elephant Body fabric is 'Strössel' by Elisabeth Dunker for Mairo.

Moopy The trouser fabric and elephant toy fabric is 'Elephants' by Carly Schwerdt for Umbrella Prints (avilable from neststudio.typepad.com). The head

{CONTINUED}

{fabric credits}

and ear fabric is 'JD-20 Chocolate Woodgrain' by Joel Dewberry for Westminster Fibers. The arm fabric is 'Measuring Tape – Cream' from the 'Building Blocks' collection by Sandy Klop of American Jane Patterns for Moda.

Piggy Bed Warmer White and pink fabric is vintage.

Maisie The spotted fabric is 'Mint Spots' by Kaffe Fassett for Rowan Fabrics. The lower body fabric is from the 'Freshcut' collection by Heather Bailey for Free Spirit Fabrics. The upper body fabric is 'Calyx' from Alexander Henry. The arm and leg fabrics are from '1930s Era Designs' for Robert Kaufman. The wool felt is from Winterwood Toys (www.winterwoodtoys.com).

Princess & the Pea The princess' body fabric is 'Cailie's Kitchen Curtains 1930–1940' from 'Patterns of History', a Kansas City Star Collection by Barbara Brackman for Moda. Blanket fabric is 'Mrs March's Collection in Antique' printed by Lecien. The pillow fabric is vintage denim. The fabric for the largest mattress is 'Aunt Grace' by Judie Rothermel & The Rocky Mountains Quilt Museum for Marcus Brothers Textiles. Other mattress fabrics include: 'Granny's Twelve' by Darlene Zimmerman for Chantclaire Fabrics; 'Star Sugar' by Kei Fabric; tea towels and vintage fabrics.

online suppliers

All of these suppliers are able to ship internationally.

AUSTRALIAN STORES

www.duckcloth.com.au
Designer fabrics including Amy Butler, as well as patterns.

www.kimoyes.com
Specialises in vintage kimono fabrics.

www.quiltfabricdelights.com.au
Quilting fabrics including Free Spirit, Amy Butler and Moda, as well as notions and other supplies.

www.retromummy.com
Specialises in cute novelty fabrics, especially import fabrics from Japan.

www.sanshi.com.au
New and vintage kimono silk fabric, modern Japanese cotton fabric, Japanese indigo-dyed fabrics (kasuri, katazome and shibori), sashiko and kogin embroidery fabric and threads, and silk screen prints from old Japanese postcards.

www.sunspun.com.au
Phone: 03 9830 1609
Fax: 03 9888 5658
Email: shop@sunspun.com.au
Quilting fabrics and supplies. They stock the entire range of Kaffe Fassett Fabrics, as well as high-quality knitting yarns in a large range of textures and colours, including Rowan. (This store only accepts orders by phone, fax or email.)

www.winterwoodtoys.com
Wool felts, including 100 per cent pure new wool felts, in a huge range of colours. They also have patterns, embroidery thread, and art and craft supplies.

INTERNATIONAL STORES

www.buntefabrics.com (US)
Specialises in colourful and fun European fabrics – particularly kids' prints – including prints from Hilco, Stenzo and Westfalen. Also has notions and patterns.

www.cathkidston.co.uk (UK)
Cath Kidston fabrics by the metre in linen, cotton and oilcloth.

{CONTINUED}

{online suppliers}

www.centerdiamond.com (US)
Fabrics and notions.

www.creationsunlimited.co.nz (New Zealand)
Patchwork fabrics, quilting accessories and notions, sewing machines and craft supplies.

www.fabrics-store.com (US)
Beautiful linens in lots of colours.

www.fatquartershop.com (US)
A large selection of fat quarter bundles and packs.

www.firesidefabrics.co.uk (UK)
Quilting fabrics from a large range of brand names such as Moda, Clothworks and Makower. Also notions and patterns.

www.hartsfabric.com (US)
Heaps of fabric including linen, denim, flannel, corduroy and kids', Asian and floral prints.

www.purlsoho.com (US)
A huge range of designer fabrics, including collections from Amy Butler, Kaffe Fassett, Denyse Schmidt and Darlene Zimmerman.

www.reprodepot.com (US)
Vintage reproduction and retro fabrics, Japanese import fabrics, as well as notions, buttons, ribbons and patterns.

www.sewmamasew.com (US)
Patterned cotton fabrics including reproduction feedsack, florals and novelty prints. Includes collections from Free Spirit, Michael Miller, Windham Fabrics, Alexander Henry, and Moda.

www.sewsos.co.uk (UK)
Patterned fabrics, interfacing, muslin and notions.

www.sewzannesfabrics.com (US)
Quilting fabrics and cute novelty kids' prints.

www.superbuzzy.com (US)
Japanese fabrics, notions and craft supplies.

www.thefatquarters.co.uk (UK)
Fabric, felt, interfacing, patterns and craft supplies.

Go to **www.penguin.com.au/softies** to download a free bonus pattern, take part in the discussion forum, and post a photograph of your creation.

VIKING

Published by the Penguin Group
Penguin Group (Australia)
250 Camberwell Road, Camberwell, Victoria 3124, Australia
(a division of Pearson Australia Group Pty Ltd)
Penguin Group (USA) Inc.
375 Hudson Street, New York, New York 10014, USA
Penguin Group (Canada)
90 Eglinton Avenue East, Suite 700, Toronto, Canada ON M4P 2Y3
(a division of Pearson Penguin Canada Inc.)
Penguin Books Ltd
80 Strand, London WC2R 0RL England
Penguin Ireland
25 St Stephen's Green, Dublin 2, Ireland
(a division of Penguin Books Ltd)
Penguin Books India Pvt Ltd
11 Community Centre, Panchsheel Park, New Delhi – 110 017, India
Penguin Group (NZ)
67 Apollo Drive, Rosedale, North Shore 0632, New Zealand
(a division of Pearson New Zealand Ltd)
Penguin Books (South Africa) (Pty) Ltd
24 Sturdee Avenue, Rosebank, Johannesburg 2196, South Africa

Penguin Books Ltd, Registered Offices: 80 Strand, London, WC2R 0RL, England

First published by Penguin Group (Australia), 2008

10 9 8 7 6 5 4 3 2 1

Cover and text design by Claire Tice © Penguin Group (Australia)
Photography by Julie Renouf
Typeset by Post Pre-press Group, Brisbane, Queensland
Colour reproduction by Splitting Image P/L, Clayton, Victoria
Printed and bound in China by 1010 Printing International Ltd

National Library of Australia
Cataloguing-in-Publication data:

More Softies
ISBN 978 0 670 07257 6 (pbk.)
1. Dollmaking. 2. Soft toys.

745.59221

penguin.com.au